SING A SONG OF SIXPENCE

A pantomime

NORMAN ROBBINS

SAMUEL

FRENCH

LONDON
NEW YORK TORONTO SYDNEY HOLLYWOOD

ISBN 0 573 06458 X

Please see page vi for further copyright information.

CHARACTERS

The Court Chamberlain of Cornucopia
Queen Dilly of Utopia
Prince Valentine, her son
Princess Rosemary of Cornucopia
Simple Simon
Dame Durdon
Witch Watt
Fairy Gossamer
Flip
Flop } **the Court Jesters of King Ferdinand**
King Ferdinand the Fourth of Cornucopia
Lucy, the maid
Zorika, a Gypsy princess
Old Meg, a Gypsy women
Rollo, Lord of the Gypsies
Squint, a Gypsy
A Ghost
Townspeople, Cooks, Guests, Gypsies, Spirits, etc.
Blackbirds and **Rabbits**

ACT I

SCENE 1 The Kingdom of Cornucopia
SCENE 2 The Witch's Lair
SCENE 3 Inside the Royal Bakery
SCENE 4 A corridor in the Royal Palace
SCENE 5 The Great Banqueting Hall
SCENE 6 A street in Cornucopia
SCENE 7 The Haunted Bedroom

ACT II

SCENE 1 The Courtyard of the Palace
SCENE 2 A Woodland Path
SCENE 3 The Gypsy Encampment
SCENE 4 A Quiet Glade
SCENE 5 Inside the Witch's Lair
SCENE 6 A Road through the Mountains
SCENE 7 The Rock of Eternity
SCENE 8 A Corridor in the Palace
SCENE 9 The Throneroom of the Palace

MUSIC

The music used in almost every production of this pantomime so far has been selected from musical comedies, operettas and popular songs of the day.

It would be impractical to attempt to list the items as the vocal capacities of different performers will vary so much. However, with a very small amount of dialogue surgery, almost any chosen number can be used with success. This also gives freedom of choice to change solo songs to duets or chorus songs, and I honestly think most Societies prefer this.

Norman Robbins

For my agents
June Epstein and Esme McKinnon
two ladies who seem to be in the middle of a permanent pantomime of their own, yet still find time to get me lots of lovely work.
Thanks, girls!

ACT I

SCENE 1

The Kingdom of Cornucopia: a typical village square

Dame Durdon's Royal Bakery is seen up R. *A small wooden bridge up* L *leads out of the Kingdom*

When the CURTAIN *rises, the townspeople are making merry. Gypsies, balloon-sellers, traders and others mingle with the crowd as they sing and dance*

SONG ONE (a)

After the song-and-dance ends, the Court Chamberlain enters from behind the Bakery, carrying a scroll and ringing a large handbell. All make way for him as he comes down C. *He hands his bell to a youth and unrolls the scroll*

Chamberlain (*reading*) Oyez, oyez, oyez! Today being the birthday of his most illustrious highness, King Ferdinand the Fourth of Cornucopia, each and every person residing in the Kingdom is invited to join the celebrations at the Palace tonight.

All cheer

The party begins at eight o'clock, so don't be late. And don't forget to bring him a present.

There is another cheer from the crowd

The Chamberlain collects his bell, rolls up his scroll and exits down L

The crowd reprise their opening song

SONG ONE (b)

As the crowd sing, they exit. As the last one does so, a loud scream is heard up L, *and Queen Dilly zooms on over the bridge, wearing roller-skates. She hurtles furiously off down* R, *shrieking wildly, and a very loud crash and shattering of glass is heard*

Prince Valentine's voice is heard off

Valentine (*anxiously*) Mother! Mother!

Queen Dilly staggers on down R *in a daze. She has one skate on and the other is missing. Her crown is lopsided and a window-frame hangs about her neck*

Dilly (*groaning*) Ooo-er.

Valentine (*hurrying to her*) Mother.

Dilly (*clutching him*) Oh, Valentine. I've been framed.

Valentine (*concerned*) Are you all right?

Dilly (*weakly*) I think so. But Woolworth's shop front will never look the same again.

Valentine Let me help you off with this. (*He takes the frame off her and hands it off*)

Dilly (*recovering*) That was all your fault, that was.

Valentine (*taken aback*) It was all *my* fault?

Dilly (*satisfied*) Ah. So you admit it, do you?

Valentine Of course I don't admit it, Mother. How on earth could it have been *my* fault?

Dilly (*prodding him*) Well it was you who said we'd have to get our skates on if we wanted to arrive here before nightfall, wasn't it?

Valentine (*laughing*) Oh, Mother, really. I didn't mean for you to take it literally. I just meant we'd have to hurry. (*Looking around*) Anyway, it looks as though we've arrived. What a funny little place it is.

Dilly If you think *this* is funny, wait till you meet old Ferdinand. You'll die laughing.

Valentine (*with a sigh*) I hardly think so, Mother. In fact I don't suppose I'll ever laugh again.

Dilly Now don't be silly, Valentine. You're not going to a funeral. You're going to be the guest of honour at a *wedding*. The victim—I mean bridegroom.

Valentine I know. That's why I'm so worried.

Dilly Worried? Worried? What on earth's there to worry about? You're the Crown Prince of Utopia, and Rosemary is Princess of Cornucopia. It'll be a perfect match.

Valentine (*protesting*) But how can I possibly marry a girl I've never seen before?

Dilly Oh, don't be so difficult, Valentine. You'll see her tonight at the reception, won't you?

Valentine (*surprised*) Reception? What reception?

Dilly Ours, of course. The minute Ferdy's got over his surprise at seeing me again, he's bound to hold a reception for us.

Valentine His surprise at seeing you again? But he's *expecting* us, isn't he?

Dilly Ah—well . . . (*She moves away cautiously*) Aha. As a matter of fact —not *exactly*. You see—I wanted it to be a sort of er—er—sort of *surprise*, so that when you proposed to Rosemary, he—er—er—he—er— wouldn't—er . . .

Valentine (*horrified*) You mean he's *not* expecting us, Mother?

Dilly Well—no. But he'll be very pleased to see us. Me. You, that is.

Valentine (*advancing on her*) Mother . .

Dilly (*skipping backwards out of his reach*) We'd better hurry along, Valentine. Mustn't keep him waiting.

Valentine Do you mean to tell me that the King doesn't know I've come here to marry his daughter?

Dilly smiles weakly and shakes her head

Oh, no, Mother. This is the end.

Dilly (*starting to cry*) I'm sorry, Valentine.

Valentine I should think so too. No wonder we had to make all our arrangements in secret. No wonder we had to walk all the way from Utopia instead of using the royal coach.

Dilly (*gushing buckets of tears*) Owwwwwwwwwwwwww!

Valentine (*with a deep sigh*) Ah, well. (*He moves to comfort her*) It can't be helped now, I suppose. We'll just have to explain everything to the King when we see him. But at least we could have used the coach and saved our feet a few blisters.

Dilly (*sniffling*) No we couldn't. We haven't got one any more.

Valentine (*baffled*) But of course we've got one, Mother. We were riding in it only last week.

Dilly I know—but I lost it to the Footman playing Happy Families.

Valentine (*stunned*) What?

Dilly That's the reason you've got to marry Rosemary. Ferdy's bound to give her a few millions for a wedding present, and then we can buy it back again, pay off all our debts, and get the crown jewels back from the pawnbrokers.

Valentine Yes, I quite understand that, but you still haven't expl—— (*He realizes*) The crown jewels? You've pawned the crown jewels?

Dilly (*sobbing afresh*) Yes.

Valentine Whatever for?

Dilly (*wailing*) To pay off the mortgage on the castle.

Valentine (*turning away*) Oh, no.

Dilly And now we're bankruptured. We haven't a penny.

Valentine Whatever are we going to *do*?

Dilly There's nothing we *can* do now unless you marry Rosemary. The baliffs are coming at midnight to throw us out. Oh, it's all my fault. (*She sobs louder*)

Valentine (*comforting her*) Never mind, Mother. It's no use crying over spilt milk.

Dilly (*sobbing louder*) And that's another thing . . .

Valentine (*quickly*) I don't think I want to hear any more. Look, why don't you run along and let King Ferdinand know we're here. I'll join you later when I've had a chance to decide what to do.

Dilly (*drying her tears*) All right, Valentine. But don't be long.

Queen Dilly exits L

Valentine Oh, what am I going to do? I'm expected to marry a girl I've never even seen before just to save us from being turned out of our own Kingdom. Oh, why was I born a prince? At least if I'd been born a commoner, I could have married the girl of my own choice. Still, it's no use being gloomy and sad about it. I'll just have to smile and hope for the best.

SONG TWO

At the end of the song, Princess Rosemary enters R *disguised as a peasant girl*

Rosemary I thought I heard someone singing.

Valentine (*seeing her*) You did, but I'm afraid I don't feel half so happy as I sounded.

Rosemary (*surprised*) A handsome young man like you with troubles? (*She smiles*) I don't believe it.

Valentine It's true though. (*Pause*) I say. Do you live here, miss? In Cornucopia?

Rosemary Why, yes. Why do you ask?

Valentine (*hesitantly*) Have—have you ever seen the Princess?

Rosemary (*solemnly*) Well—yes. In fact I see her every day.

Valentine (*pleased*) You do? What a stroke of luck. You see I've come here to propose to her, but I've no idea what she looks like.

Rosemary I see. So you're another one, are you. Someone else who's heard about the Magic Crown.

Valentine (*puzzled*) Magic Crown? I don't understand.

Rosemary The Magic Crown that the Fairy Queen gave to my fa——I mean to King Ferdinand.

Valentine I'm sorry. I don't know what you're talking about.

Rosemary So long as the Magic Crown is in the King's possession, the land will be free of giants, witches and goblins, and all the gold in his counting-house will double itself in quantity every night. But should anyone *steal* the Crown, then a terrible disaster will befall him.

Valentine Surely you don't think that *I'd* want to steal it?

Rosemary No. But you might have come here to marry his daughter in the hope of getting your hands on his money.

Valentine (*sadly*) You're right. That's exactly why I've come.

Rosemary Oh. (*Sadly*) Just like all the others.

Valentine (*quickly*) Not for myself, you understand. It's for my mother. Queen Dilly of Utopia.

Rosemary (*surprised*) Queen Dilly? Then *you* must be Valentine?

Valentine (*taken aback*) That's right. But how did you know?

Rosemary Oh—I've *heard* about you. That's all.

Valentine Well—I suppose I'd better be getting along to the palace. They're bound to be expecting me now. Still, if what you say is true, I don't suppose the Princess will even listen to my proposal.

Rosemary She—might. Under certain circumstances.

Valentine Do you think so? Honestly?

Rosemary Faint heart ne'er won fair lady.

Valentine I suppose not. (*Thinking*) But I've never proposed to anyone before, and I'm not at all sure of how to go about it. (*He hesitates*) Would—would you mind if—if—well, if I practised my proposal on you?

Rosemary I'd be delighted.

Valentine (*clearing his throat*) Er. Fair Princess. (*He kneels*) Let thy radiant eyes fall upon me, Prince Valentine of Utopia, and love's flame light in your heart . . .

Rosemary (*beginning to laugh*) Oh, dear.

Valentine (*rising*) I'm sorry you find it so amusing.

Rosemary (*laughing gaily*) I'm sorry, but it sounded so funny.

Valentine (*coldly*) Indeed? (*He begins to see the funny side of it*) Well—I suppose it *did*. (*He laughs with her*) Thank goodness the Princess didn't hear me.

Rosemary But she *did*. *I'm* the Princess.

Valentine (*stunned*) You?

Rosemary (*still laughing*) Princess Rosemary Angela of Cornucopia, at your service. (*She curtsies to him*)

Valentine But—but—if you're *really* the Princess, what on earth are you doing walking around the streets in peasant clothing?

Rosemary I often dress like this when I want to visit my people unnoticed. They think I'm just a serving-girl from the palace.

Valentine A serving-girl? They must be blind. How could they *not* recognize true royalty beneath those simple clothes?

Rosemary Well *you* didn't.

Valentine (*laughing*) You're right, but now that I've met you at last, I'll never let you go.

SONG THREE

After the song, Valentine and Rosemary exit L. *As they do so, Simple Simon enters* R

Simon (*singing*) I've got sixpence, jolly, jolly sixpence.
I've got sixpence, to last me all my life.
I've twopence to lend, and twopence to spend,
And twopence to take home to my wife. Pom, pom, pom.

(*He scratches his head*) Here—wait a minute. Twopence to take home to my wife? But I'm not married, am I? In that case I've got *fourpence* to spend. And as for *lending* twopence—well—I've got nobody to lend it to, so that means I've got a whole *sixpence* to spend. Coo, it must be my lucky day. A whole sixpence. (*He holds it up to show, but it slips out of his fingers and falls*) Oh—it's dropped down that drain. Now I've got nothing to spend. Talk about rotten luck. (*He sees the audience*) Oh—hello. Are you all enjoying yourselves? Oh—I'm sorry about that, but you're not getting your money back. We've used it to buy a jar of coffee. (*He laughs*) I'd better introduce myself, hadn't I? (*He recites*)

My name is Simple Simon (as in the rhyme you're told),
One day I met a Pieman, and feeling rather bold,
I said "I have no penny, but can I taste your ware?"
And he said, "Get out of it, you scruffy-looking twerp!"

Oh, he wasn't *nice*. Still, I didn't really mind. I get all my pies for nothing anyway. From old Dame Durdon. She has the bakehouse over there. (*He indicates*) She makes lovely pies, does Dame Durdon. Great big *crusty* ones. Full of meat and gravy. (*He licks his lips*) Have you met her yet? Oh, you will.

Dame Durdon enters behind him from the bakery

She's an ugly looking old faggot. You can't miss her. (*He chuckles*) She's got so many chins, her eyes look like two sultanas peering over a pile of pancakes. (*He laughs*)

Dame Durdon creeps down behind him

She's had her face lifted so many times, her nose is half way down her back. (*He laughs*) She tried to put some beauty cream on her face last night, but it kept backing down the tube. (*He falls about with laughter then sees the Dame*) Ooooer!

Dame So. I'm an ugly old faggot am I? (*She rolls up her sleeves*)
Simon (*Backing away*) No. No.
Dame (*advancing on him*) Stand still while I hit you.
Simon Wait. Wait. Chloë. Don't hit me. I was only joking. I knew you were there all the time.
Dame You did?
Simon Of course I did. I was just pulling your leg.
Dame You were?
Simon Yes. The minute you opened that bakehouse door, I got a whiff of that lovely cooking, and I knew you were right behind me.
Dame Oh, Simon.
Simon (*sniffing*) And talking about smells . . . (*He looks at the soles of his shoes*)
Dame (*preening herself*) Oh——you've noticed it, have you?
Simon Eh?
Dame My new perfume. Ashes of Cucumber.
Simon I thought it was fly killer.
Dame It's scent. Scent from Paris.
Simon I should send it back again if I were you.
Dame What?
Simon I'm only joking again. You can take a joke, can't you?
Dame Of course I can. I've got you, haven't I?
Simon Are we friends again, now, Chloë?
Dame (*girlishly*) Well—all right. And just to show there's no hard feelings, you can give me a big, big kiss. (*She puckers her lips*)
Simon (*squirming*) Oh, Chloë. I can't kiss you just now. Not with all these people watching. Can't I do it later?
Dame Oh, come on. They won't mind.
Simon But I'm shy.
Dame Don't be silly. Kiss me here in front of the bakery.
Simon No.
Dame Go on. Oh, all right then. If you won't kiss me in front of the bakery, we'll go round the back and you can kiss me behind.
Simon Here—talking about the bakery. Have you finished all the stuff for

the King's party tonight? Now you're Official Caterer to the palace, you'll have a lot to do, won't you?

Dame (*putting her hand to her mouth*) You're right. And there's a mountain of things to make. I'd better go get cracking. (*She turns to exit*)

Simon (*swaggering away*) Saved again.

Dame (*grabbing him*) And don't think you're going to be stood standing about out here doing nothing while I'm up to me ear-holes in pastry. There's work to be done and you're going to do some of it. (*Taking his ear*) We've eight hundred apple pies to make, and *you* can peel the apples.

She drags him off into the bakery, as

the CURTAIN *falls*

SCENE 2

The Witch's Lair. A dark blackcloth, lit with blue light

Witch Watt stands L, *lit with a green light, gazing into a crystal ball*

Witch A birthday party for the King;
Do my ears inform me right?
Then now's my chance. His Magic Crown
Is mine this very night.
A birthday present *I'll* send too;
A really wond'rous sight;
But the gift *I* send unto the King
Will put him in a sorry plight.

She produces a small bag of rye from her gown

For with this pocketful of rye,
I'll have made a *special* pie.
Filled with blackbirds, sweet of song,
To make the Palace sleep ere long;
And whilst they lie in slumber deep
Away with the Magic Crown I'll creep.
With its powers mine, I'll rule supreme.
At long, long last, I live my dream. (*She cackles with glee*)

Fairy Gossamer enters R *in a white light*

Fairy Oh, evil Witch, your plan will fail.
A *happy* end there'll be to this tale.
Your powers fail against aught good.

Witch (*angrily*) Bah! Enough from you I've stood.
I fear you not. I fear not good.

Fairy (*smiling*) Then do your worst. But very soon
I promise you, you'll meet your doom.
You'll meet your match in Valentine!
Witch (*snarling*) I'll deal with *him* when I have time.
Fairy Take care he does not deal with thee.
Witch Don't make me laugh.
Fairy You'll see. You'll see.

Fairy Gossamer exits R

Witch You stupid fool to threaten *me*;
The Witch of Ancient Days.
The one to whom the stars bow down——
Whose voice the wind obeys.
I who'd lived ten thousand years before *you* first saw light.
You think to beat such power as mine
In the space of one short night?
No, no, my stupid fairy friend, *I'll* deal with Valentine.
And ere the sun's light brings the dawn,
The Magic Crown is *mine*! (*She shrieks with laughter*)

The Lights fade to a Black-out

SCENE 3

Inside the Royal Bakery—the kitchen

On a long table at the back stand a large baking-bowl, bag of flour, wooden spoon, rolling-pin and a large lump of "cod" pastry. Under the table and hidden from view is a large tin marked "Currants", a small handbrush and a large packet of soap powder. To one side is a huge oven

The Assistant Cooks are busy with their bowls and spoons mixing cakes, etc., for the party, and dancing or singing

SONG FOUR

As the song ends, Dame Durdon enters L *in her cook's outfit. She carries a list*

Cooks Good morning, Dame Durdon.
Dame I'll give you good morning if you don't stop messing about and get on with some work. Singing and dancing at this time of day. What's the matter with you?
Boy Haven't you *heard*?
Dame Heard? Heard what?
Boy The news, of course. They're going to choose the prettiest woman in the kingdom to present our birthday gift to the King tonight.
Dame (*fluttering*) Oh. Opportunity knocks at last. Quick. Ring up the—(*local hairdressing salon*)—and make me an appointment.

Girl Whatever for?

Dame What do you mean "Whatever for"? Didn't you hear what he just said? They're looking for someone to present a birthday gift to the King tonight.

Girl Yes—but he also said "someone *pretty*".

The Cooks laugh

Dame And just what's *that* supposed to mean? Aren't *I* pretty?

Boy Yes. Pretty ugly.

The Cooks laugh

Dame (*angrily*) That's done it. Come here. (*She advances on him*)

Boy (*hopping out of reach*) Calm down, Dame Durdon. We're only teasing you. You're the one they've chosen to do it. After all—Simon tells us you once won a beauty competition.

Dame (*preening*) Oh, he shouldn't have done. But it's true. I won the first beauty competition that this kingdom ever had. (*She simpers*) And you'll *never* guess who crowned me.

Boy Moses?

The Cooks rock with laughter. Dame Durdon is furious. She grabs the pastry from the table and, waving it like a flail, chases them all off

The Cooks exit

Dame Durdon hurls the pastry after one of them

Dame Cheeky monkeys. (*She picks up the pastry*) Oh, look at it. It's filthy. (*She rubs it down the front of her dress, spits on a bad patch and rubs it with her finger*) That'll do. (*She puts it back on the table*) Now—where's me list? (*She finds it and peers at it*) Eight hundred apple pies. Five hundred apricot tarts. Six hundred swiss rolls. Five hundred pork pies. A cooks' special. (*Blankly*) A cooks' special? Oh, I wonder what I can give 'em? I've done some fantastic things with an Oxo cube and a couple of kipper fillets, you know. Wait a minute. I know. I'll give 'em some fried centipede. (*To the audience*) Have you tried it? Fried centipede? It doesn't taste very nice, but at least everybody gets a leg. (*Back to the list*) Now what else is there? A giant size currant cake. Yes—well I'd better get on with that, hadn't I? Where's me wooden spoon? (*She shakes flour into the bowl*) Flour. Eggs. (*She throws some egg boxes into the bowl*) Currants. (*She gets the tin from under the table and looks inside it*) Hmm. Funny-looking currants. (*She pours them into the bowl*) Oh, I do like making cakes. (*She stirs*)

Simon enters down L *holding a stick with a line and a bent pin attached, plus a jamjar on strings. He is wearing a sou'-wester and oilskins. He crosses in front of her jauntily*

Simon Ta ta, Chloë.

Dame Hoy. Hoy. Hoy.

Simon stops and looks at her

And where do you think *you're* going, John West?

Simon Fishing.

Dame Oh—*fishing*. (*To the audience*) He's going fishing.

Simon Yes, I am. Oh—and by the way. You haven't seen my tin of flies, anywhere, have you?

Dame Flies? What do you want flies for?

Simon To go fishing with, of course.

Dame Why? Are you that hard up for company?

Simon No, no. You don't understand, Chloë. They're to put on the end of my line. To attract the fish.

Dame Ohhhhhhh, I see. The flies are to attract the fish.

Simon (*happily*) That's right.

Dame And you're quite sure about that, are you? That it's the flies that attract them? You don't think it might perhaps be the *worm*.

Simon (*blankly*) Worm? What worm?

Dame (*grimly*) The worm that's holding on to the other end of the fishing rod. (*She tears over to him and snatches the rod out of his hand*) Give me that.

Simon Why? Do you want to go fishing as well?

Dame (*throwing the rod off*) No, I do not want to go fishing as well. And neither do you. You're going to stop stood standing right here until we've got all this work finished. Understand?

Simon (*shrugging*) Oh, all right then. There's no use going anyway if I can't find my flies. Are you sure you haven't seen 'em?

Dame (*moving back to the table*) No I haven't. Where did you leave 'em? (*She picks up the currant tin*)

Simon In a big tin marked currants.

Dame Well that's a daft place to leave flies anyway. In a big tin marked . . . (*Realizing*) *Currants*.

Simon (*spotting the tin*) Oh—you've found 'em.

Dame (*spluttering*) Found 'em? You stupid little twerp. I've just put 'em into this cake I'm baking. Folks might have eaten'em.

Simon Oh, that's all right, Chloë. There's no need to get excited. It wouldn't have done 'em any harm. They were all dead ones.

Dame (*grabbing the pastry again*) Gerrout! (*She swipes at him with it, and it falls to the floor again.*)

Simon dashes off

Look what you've made me do now. (*She picks up the pastry and wipes it down with the handbrush*) Oh, what am I going to do with this lot?

Witch Watt enters L *in a green light*

Witch Pssss. Psss.

Dame (*turning*) A gas leak. (*She sees the Witch and reacts*) Oh—it's . . . (*any well-known personality*)

Witch Fool. I am Witch Watt.

Dame I don't care if you're which-way-is-it-to-the-Town-Hall, missis. You can just get out of here. Your face is curdling me cream cakes.

Witch (*fiercely*) Silence! I come to seek your aid.

Dame (*wide-eyed*) I didn't know I'd lost it.

Witch I want you to make me a pie—rich and tender. In fact—a pie fit for a king. (*She shrieks with fiendish laughter*)

Dame (*in cultured tones*) You've just been "Listening with Mother".

Witch (*grabbing her*) Well? Will you do it?

Dame Oooer. Well—I don't know. I've never made a pie for a witch before. (*Realizing*) A witch? Here—you're not supposed to be here. Witches aren't allowed . . .

The Witch makes magic signs with her hands, and Dame Durdon goes glassy eyed

Witch Take this bag of magic rye—(*producing it from her robes*)—and include it in the mixture. (*She hands it to her*) Now—

To your work go right away.
I'll call for the pie—later today.

The Witch screams with laughter and exits L

Dame (*coming round*) Oh—I feel all of a tizwas. I can't remember what I was doing. (*She looks at the bag of rye*) Oh—yes. I remember. I was going to make a pie for that sweet little old lady who just went out. (*She shakes her head to clear it*) I'd better go get another bowl.

Dame Durdon exits R

Flip (*off*) Coo-ee. Dame Durdon?

Flop (*off*) Coo-ee.

Flip and Flop, the Court Jesters, enter. They are in bright suits with cap and bells

Flip (*looking round*) There's nobody here. It's empty.

Flop Do you think we've come to the right place, Flip?

Flip Of course we have, Flop. Can't you see all those baking things and that enormous oven over there? I bet you could cook an elephant in that.

Flop Oh, don't talk to me about cooking. It reminds me of when I lived in lodgings, and the landlady kept animals at the back of the house.

Flip What happened?

Flop Well—the first day I was there, one of the *chickens* died, so we all had chicken soup for dinner. The next day, the *pig* died, so we all had pork chops. The following day, the *cow* died, so we all had rib of beef.

Flip What's wrong with that?

Flop Nothing. But the day after, her *husband* died—so I left.

Flip snatches off his cap and hits Flop with it

Flip I might have expected something like that from a half-wit like you. No wonder they want you to be Mastoid of Ceremonies at the party tonight.

Flop You mean *Master* of Ceremonies, Flip. A mastoid is a pain in the ear.

Flip Well, you said it.

Flop I'm fed up of you taking the micky out of me all the time. People like me don't grow on trees, you know.

Flip No—they're usually *swinging* from them.

Flop Is that so? Well let me tell you. If it wasn't for *my* brains, we wouldn't be working for the King at all.

Flip *Your* brains? That's a laugh. If brains were gunpowder, you wouldn't have enough to blow your hat off.

Flop Oh no? Well just you try me. Ask me a question and I'll show you whether I've got any brains or not. Go on. Ask me.

Flip All right then. I'll ask you a question on history. What would you expect to find in Ancient Greece?

Flop Simple. Old fish and chips.

Flip hits him with his cap again

Flip Oh, it's useless trying to get any sense out of you. Let's get on with what we're supposed to be doing. Now we came here to see if Dame Durdon had finished all the goodies for the King's birthday party, didn't we?

Flop Yes.

Flip But Dame Durdon isn't here to ask, is she?

Flop No.

Flip So what are we going to do?

Flop Look in the oven and see what's inside it.

Flip Right.

They cross to the oven, open it and look inside

Flop I can't see anything, can you?

Flip Not a sausage.

Flop Tell you what. I'll climb inside and have a closer look.

Flip No. We'll *both* climb in. After all. Two heads are better than one.

Flip and Flop climb into the oven

Dame Durdon enters with a fresh bowl

Dame Who's left my oven door open? They'll let all the heat out. (*She slams it shut*) Now then. One rye pie, coming up. (*She puts the bowl down and begins to roll the pastry. It falls to the floor. She picks it up, scrubs the table legs with it, etc., then dusts it down with Daz from under the table*) There. Whiter than white again.

Simon enters

Simon I'm back.
Dame I can see that. I thought you were going fishing.
Simon I was, but I changed my mind.
Dame About time, too. If it had been mine, I'd have changed it years ago and got one that worked.
Simon (*lifting the pastry*) What are you doing?
Dame I'll do you, if you don't put that down. Gerroff! (*She grabs the pastry*)
Simon Don't snatch. (*He tugs it back*)

They tug at the pastry till Simon lets go and Dame Durdon falls backwards with a yell

Dame Ooooooooooooh.

Simon exits quickly

Help! Help! I've twisted my vertigo. I'm dying. Help!

Rosemary and Valentine enter

Rosemary Dame Durdon. Whatever's the matter? (*She runs to her*)
Valentine We thought you were being attacked. (*He helps her up*)
Dame (*furiously*) Where is he? Let me get at him.
Rosemary (*bewildered*) Who? What's happened?
Dame What's happened? What's happened? I was nearly murdered in my bed. That's what happened.
Rosemary (*anxiously*) But you're all right, aren't you? You're not hurt?
Dame Hurt? I've nearly knotted my sacariliac. I feel like I've been ... (*She notices Valentine for the first time*) Ohhhhh ... (*She flutters her eyelashes*) Who's this?
Valentine Prince Valentine. At your service. (*He bows*)
Dame *Prince* Valentine? Ohhhh. A real live Prince. There hasn't been one of them in Cornucopia since I was a young girl like you, Rosemary.
Rosemary (*interested*) Oh? Which Prince was that?
Dame (*wistfully*) You wouldn't know him, my dear. It was long before your time. He came to Cornucopia to find a bride, met me, swept me off me feet and told me I was the girl of his dreams.
Rosemary How romantic. And what happened?
Dame He married my sister. I've never seen him since. (*She begins to sniffle*)
Valentine (*handing her his handkerchief*) Poor Dame Durdon. How unhappy you must have been.
Dame Yes, but I bet I wasn't half so unhappy as *she* was when they left for their honeymoon.
Rosemary Why's that?
Dame I'd soaked her false teeth in ready-mixed concrete. (*She shrugs*) Still—I soon got over it. I had to do. I had you to look after, didn't I? (*She puts her arm around Rosemary*)

Rosemary (*to Valentine*) Dame Durdon was my nursemaid until I grew old enough to look after myself. Now she runs the Royal Bakery.

Valentine (*to Dame*) So you never married, I suppose?

Dame No. But I've not been neglected. It's just that every time I get my hooks into somebody, I think better of it or something goes wrong. Shall I tell you about it?

Valentine
Rosemary } Please do. (*Speaking together*)

SONG FIVE

At the end of the song, there is a loud scream from inside the oven. All react

Rosemary What was that?

Dame It came from inside the oven.

Valentine Quick! Open it up!

They fling open the oven door

Two tiny tots with bright red faces, dressed in the Jester costumes of Flip and Flop, scuttle out and exit

Dame Durdon faints into Valentine's arms, as the Lights fade to a Black-out and—

The CURTAIN *falls*

SCENE 4

A corridor in the Royal Palace. Darkness

The Witch enters L *in a green light*

Witch (*after a shriek of evil laughter*)
The spell I laid is duly cast.
The pie begins to grow.
And to this Royal Palace
That dainty dish shall go.
To prove unto his Majesty
Who really *is* the master.
Once opened, then the pie reveals
Its message of disaster.

The Witch laughs and exits L

Chamberlain (*off*) Your Majesty. Your Majesty. Wait.

King Ferdinand enters R, *almost in tears, followed by the anxious Chamberlain*

King (*waving his arms in the air*) No, no, no. Send her away. I won't have her coming here and ruining my birthday party. Tell her I've gone to Australia, or something.

The Chamberlain begins to exit

No—come back. What does she want?

The Chamberlain tries to speak

It doesn't matter. She can't have it. Oh, why did she have to pick today of *all* days? Twenty years without a word from her—and now this. What a birthday present! Well, don't just stand there. Get rid of her. Tell her I've got the measles.

The Chamberlain turns to go

Oh, what's the use? She'll never believe you. (*With great woe*) What have I done to deserve this?

Chamberlain Is there anything *I* can do to help, sire?

King Nothing can help me now—unless she falls into the moat. (*Brightening*) Now *there*'s an idea.

Chamberlain I'll go raise the drawbridge, sire.

King No. It's no use. She can swim.

Chamberlain If I might suggest, sire? Perhaps . . .

King (*shaking his head*) Wouldn't work.

Chamberlain Then how about . . .

King Too risky.

Chamberlain But what if . . .

King It's hopeless. I've tried them all before. What we really need is something *drastic*.

Chamberlain (*suddenly*) I've *got* it.

King (*edging away*) Is it catching?

Chamberlain No, no, sire. But I have it all the same. MICE!

King Mice?

Chamberlain Mice.

King Have you seen a vet about it?

Chamberlain You don't understand, sire. Tell her that the palace is overrun with mice. She'll be so terrified, she'll leave at once.

King If you knew her like I know her, you'd realize that as soon as the mice know she's in the palace, it'd be *them* who'd be leaving.

Dilly (*off*) Yoo-hoo, darling. I'm here.

King Trapped. (*He kneels on the floor behind the Chamberlain and covers his head with his cloak*)

Dilly enters with a large suitcase

Dilly Peek-a-boo! (*She slaps him on the bottom*) What are you doing down there, Ferdinand?

King (*sourly*) Getting up. (*He does so*)

Dilly I can see that, silly. But what were you doing down there in the first place?

King (*feeling foolish*) Well—I—er—er . . .

Dilly (*pinching his cheek*) Don't be bashful. Tell Dilly.

King (*annoyed*) Well if you *must* know—I was trying to *hide*.

Dilly (*delightedly*) How *quaint*. (*She hands the suitcase to the Chamberlain*) Still as shy as ever. (*To the Chamberlain*) I remember when he used to come to our house to see me. He always pretended he was visiting my sister, but I knew it was me he fancied all along. (*To the King*) Wasn't it, you naughty old thing?

King (*fiercely*) No, it was not.

Dilly (*wagging her finger at him*) Ahhhh. And by the way, whatever happened to the poor old thing? I haven't laid eyes on her since I married Henry.

King As a matter of fact, she's the owner of the Royal Bakery, and keeps us supplied with cakes and pastries.

Dilly How *lovely* for her. She always did like burning things. Now I'll just go unpack before I pop down to see her again. A little matter of ready-mixed concrete.

King (*quickly*) Oh, there's no need for you to unpack. She'll be here tonight, so you'll have plenty of time to see her before you catch the last coach back to Utopia.

Dilly Oh, I'm not going back just yet, Ferdinand. I've only just arrived, and we've got lots to talk about. Like money, gold, jewels and hard cash. Furs, feathers, new hats, shoes, handbags, dresses, stockings—oh, the list's *endless*. I'll be here for *weeks*. (*She takes back her case*)

King (*in a panic*) But you can't. I mean—no. It's impossible. Out of the question.

Dilly It is?

King Of course it is. You can't possibly stay here in the palace. We've got *mice*.

Dilly (*beaming*) I *thought* you might have. (*She opens her case*) So I came prepared. (*She produces an enormous mouse-trap*) Better luck next time.

Dilly exits

King (*groaning*) That's torn it. She won't budge now. We'll *never* get rid of her. What am I going to do?

Flip and Flop enter

Ah. Just the men I'm looking for.

Flip }
Flop } (*Speaking together*) Who? Us?

King I need a miracle worker.

Flip (*pushing Flop forward*) The very man.

King (*peering at Flop*) Him? Are you sure?

Flip I'm positive. The day he does a stroke of work—it'll be a miracle.

King This is no time for joking. The country is facing a national disaster.

Queen Dilly's arrived from Utopia, and unless we can get rid of her quickly, we'll be as penniless as she is.

Chamberlain Not so long as you have the Magic Crown, sire.

King Magic Crown? Leave it alone with that woman for two minutes, Chamberlain, and she'll be organizing a *raffle* for it. No. She's got to go.

Chamberlain Perhaps she'd listen to reason, sire.

King Listen to reason? The only time that woman ever listens to anything is when it's *money* talking. It's no wonder they've nicknamed her "Resolution".

Flop Resolution?

King Yes. She gets harder to keep every day. (*In despair*) Oh what are we going to do about her?

Flip Why not try to frighten her away?

King (*delighted*) Brilliant idea. Chamberlain. Quick. Go hang a large mirror on her wall.

Flip No, no, sire. Put her in the haunted bedroom.

King Haunted bedroom? (*To the Chamberlain*) Do we have one?

Chamberlain (*nervously*) Yes, your Majesty. But it's a terrible place. No one has ever gone into it and remained sane. They all go mad.

King You mean—it's like the Houses of Parliament? Then that's just what we want. See to it at once, Chamberlain. It's the haunted bedroom for her.

The Chamberlain exits nervously

Ho ho. I feel quite happy now. By this time tomorrow, she'll be miles away. Bravo, my loyal Jesters. I'll see your wages are raised for this.

The King and the Jesters dance a figure of eight with linked arms

During the dance the Witch enters L, *in a green light*

Witch Laugh while ye may. Dance and sing.
For woe to your kingdom this day I'll bring.

They stop dancing in shock, and recoil

Make merry, you fools. Like children play.
For I promise you'll smile no more from today.

Fairy Gossamer enters R, *in a white light*

Fairy Heed not her words. Fear not her power;
For I'm always near in danger's hour,
With legions of fairies to guard your lands
From such evil folks and their demon bands.

Witch Bah. You can do naught to stay their plight.

Fairy Begone, I command you. I banish you with light!

A white light is directed on to the Witch

The Witch screams, recoils, and exits L

King (*terrified*) Ohhhhh!
Fairy Fear not, O King, but take this advice.
Trust nothing that's made of sugar and spice.
King (*bewildered*) I don't understand. Do you mean I've got to go on a diet?
Fairy In just a while 'twill be quite clear,
But a Champion you will find right here,
Within these very palace walls. So quickly,
Ere the evening falls, for then it is that witch's work
Is carried out. Grim dangers lurk,
And evil spreads its night black wings.
Now go! Remember all these things.
Beware strange gifts. Protect your Crown,
Or your palace and kingdom come tumbling down!

Fairy Gossamer exits R

King (*weakly*) This is all Dilly's fault. Everything was all right before she came. Oh, what a terrible birthday I'm having.

With Flip and Flop supporting him, the King totters off R. *As they exit, Valentine and Rosemary enter* L

Rosemary Here we are. Welcome to the Royal Palace.
Valentine Why, thank you, your Highness. (*He gives her a deep bow*)
Rosemary (*looking around*) I wonder where everyone is?
Valentine It's certainly very quiet.
Rosemary It won't stay that way for long. Once Father's party begins, you won't be able to hear yourself think. They get noisier every year. Now I'd better go and change before I introduce you to him. He'd have a fit if he saw me dressed like this. I won't be long.

Rosemary exits R

Valentine What a wonderful girl she's turned out to be. I was a fool to worry. I couldn't have found anyone half so beautiful if I'd searched the entire world.

SONG AND DANCE SIX

After the song, Valentine exits R. *As he does so, Simon and Dame Durdon enter* L *in their finery*

Simon (*peering around*) Isn't it quiet?
Dame Pardon?
Simon (*louder*) Quiet.
Dame Don't you tell me to be quiet, or I'll dot you one.
Simon I wasn't telling you to be quiet, Chloë. I said it sounded quiet.

Dame What do you mean, "sounded quiet"? If it's quiet, there isn't any sound.

Simon I know there isn't. That's what I just said. It sounds quiet.

Dame (*loudly*) It *doesn't* sound quiet.

Simon I'm not surprised with you making all that noise.

Dame (*disgustedly*) Oh, I give up. What time is it, useless? Perhaps we're too early.

Simon I don't know. I haven't got a watch.

Dame (*amazed*) Haven't got a watch? Oh, well, we can soon alter that, can't we? I'll sell you one.

Simon (*surprised*) You'll sell me one? For how much?

Dame If it was anybody else, seventy-nine pence, but as it's you, you can have it for a pound.

Simon Right. You're on. (*He hands over a pound note*)

Dame (*producing a watch out of her bag as she takes the cash*) And here's your watch.

Simon (*taking it*) Ta. (*He examines it*) Here—this is a *chocolate* watch. It won't go!

Dame Of *course* it'll go. Just give me another pound, and I'll prove it to you.

Simon Oh, all right. (*He hands over another pound*) Now then. What do I have to do to make it go?

Dame *Suck* it. (*She chortles with laughter*)

Simon (*aside*) Oh, heck. I'll have to get that money back from her. (*To the Dame*) Here, I say. I bet you two pounds I can put this watch where I can see it, the audience can see it, but *you* can't.

Dame Oh, I'm not falling for that old gag. You'll put it behind my back.

Simon No I won't. Honest.

Dame All right then. (*She puts two pounds on the floor*) There's my two pounds.

Simon And here's mine. (*He puts two pounds down*) Now I'm going to put this where I can see it, the audience can see it, but you can't. All right?

Dame Off you go.

Simon places the watch on top of Dame Durdon's head

Simon There you are. I can see it, they can see it, but you can't. I win. (*He bends to pick up the cash*)

Dame Wait a minute. Wait a minute. (*She takes a mirror out of her bag and peers into it*) I can see it perfectly through this mirror. I win. (*She scoops up the money*)

Dilly enters R *behind Dame Durdon*

Dilly (*spotting her*) Ah, woman. Go tell the King I'm ready for him.

Dame (*turning*) Don't you "woman" me, you—you . . . (*She recognizes her*) DILLY!

Dilly (*recognizing her*) Chloë. My little twister . . . I mean, sister. (*She embraces her*)

Dame I thought I'd never see you again—with a bit of luck.

Dilly Naughty. (*She links arms with her and they move* L) Oh, you must come up to my room and tell me all the news. There must be lots of people we can tear to shreds.

Dame (*as they begin to exit*) Well I must tell you. I had a letter from Cinders the other day, and that Prince Charming hasn't turned out to be the catch she thought he was going to be. As a matter of fact . . .

Dilly and Dame Durdon exit L, *their voices fading*

Simon (*looking after them*) Well now we know what happened to the Ugly Sisters. Oh, I'm fed up with women, I am.

The King, the Chamberlain, Flip and Flop enter R

All Us too.

SONG AND DANCE SEVEN

After the song, all exit but Simon. Lucy, the maid, enters with a clothes basket. She passes Simon who reacts

Simon Hey. Missis. Just a minute.

Lucy stops and looks at him

Where have *you* been all my life?

Lucy Well for *half* of it, I wasn't even *born*. (*She turns to go*)

Simon Har, har. Very funny. Well just you wait, Missis Maid. Just you wait till I get my new Royls Rolce and it's pouring with rain, and you're waiting for a bus and I'm driving past. I shan't stop and ask *you* if you want a lift.

Lucy It wouldn't be much use to me if you did. I live in a *bungalow*.

Lucy exits

Simon (*gasping*) She lives in a bungalow. (*He shouts off after her*) Hey!

Lucy enters

What are you doing, anyway?

Lucy Well if you must know, I'm going into the garden to hang out the clothes.

Simon Oh, can I help you? I'm ever so good at doing things like that. What would you like me to hang first?

Lucy You could make a start with yourself.

Simon (*beginning to cry*) It's not fair. Everybody picks on me.

Lucy (*feeling sorry*) Oh, I'm sorry. (*She puts the basket down*) I didn't mean to be unkind. Please don't cry.

Simon I can't help it. Nobody wants me.

Lucy Don't say that.

Simon It's true. I'm just the village idiot.
Lucy You're *not*
Simon I am.
Lucy You're *not.*
Simon I am. (*Pause*) Aren't you going to say I'm not?
Lucy (*laughing*) All right. You're not. Now come on, dry those eyes and let's see you smiling again.

Simon flashes a huge smile

Simon You're quite nice, really, aren't you? What's your name?
Lucy Guess.
Simon (*puzzled*) That's a funny name.
Lucy I mean, try to guess what it is, silly.
Simon Well will you give me a kiss if I get it right?
Lucy Will I what?

SONG EIGHT

At the end of the song, Lucy gives Simon a quick kiss on the cheek, picks up her basket and exits L. *The Chamberlain enters* R

Chamberlain (*loudly*) The party is about to begin, sir. The guests are assembled in the Great Hall.
Simon Righty-ho, cock. Let the battle commence.

The Chamberlain and Simon exit

Scene 5

The Great Banqueting Hall

There is a throne for the King, and a large screen behind which the giant pie is set

A stately gavotte or minuet is in progress, and all the guests are assembled. Footmen move around serving drinks, food, etc. At the end of the number (*a few bars only*) *the King steps forward*

King Welcome, my loyal subjects. Welcome to my party. Now before we go any further, I should just like to say . . . (*He sees the screen that conceals the pie*) What's *that*? (*He points*)
Chamberlain It's a screen, sire.
King I know that, blockhead. But what's it doing there?
Chamberlain (*baffled*) I don't know, sire. It wasn't there five minutes ago.
King Then have it removed. Immediately!
Chamberlain Very good, sire.

The Chamberlain claps his hands. Two footmen remove the screen to reveal the giant pie. All react

Valentine (*stepping forward*) It's a pie. A giant pie.
King Where did it come from?

Dame Well it didn't come out of *my* bakehouse.
Rosemary Oh, Valentine. I don't like it.
Simon You haven't tasted it, yet.
Rosemary There's something strange about it. Oh, Daddy. I'm afraid.
Valentine (*holding her*) There's nothing to be afraid of. I promise you.
King I wonder what's inside it?
Dilly A herd of cows by the look of it.
Simon It might be a *bomb*.

Everyone but Dilly moves back quickly

Dilly Don't be silly. Bombs haven't been invented yet.
Flip Well isn't someone going to open it?
King Good idea. Chamberlain—open the pie.
Chamberlain But—but . . . What if it *is* a bomb, sire? They could have invented them *today*.
King Hmmm. You might be right, there, Chamberlain. You might be right.
Chamberlain (*quickly*) And anyway—I've got a bad leg. (*He limps*)
Dilly Well you aren't going to open it with your leg, are you? Honestly, you men. You're all afraid. Well, I'm not. No pie's going to get the better of me. It's going to be opened this very minute. Right *now*.
Valentine What are you going to do, Mother?
Dilly I'll show you what I'm going to do. Flop, open that pie.
Flop (*quaking*) *Me?*
Simon Yes. Go on.
Flop Why don't *you* do it?
Simon Because it's against my religion. I'm a devout coward.
King Well, get on with it, somebody. We can't stand about all night just looking at the thing.
Valentine I'll open it. (*Steps forward*)
Rosemary No. (*She tries to pull him back*)
Dilly Stand back. I'll do it myself. (*She goes up to the pie*) Oh. There's a little note attached to it. (*She reads*)

To wish you happy birthday,
I've sent you something nice.
A dainty dish, fit for a king,
And packed with sugar and spice.

King Sugar and spice?
Dilly Oh, we can open it after all.
King (*remembering*) No. No. You mustn't. Stop her.
Dilly (*heaving up the crust*) Come on, everybody. Line up for a slice.
King (*wailing*) Too late.

There is a great roll of thunder and the lights flicker

Rosemary What's happening?
King It's the curse. (*He totters to his throne and collapses on it*)
Dilly (*staggering back*) There's something coming out.

Everyone falls back as the Four and Twenty Blackbirds emerge from the pie and begin to dance and sing

SONG NINE

At first all are delighted, but as the song and dance continue, they begin to fall into a deep sleep. By the time the music ends, all are snoring quietly in heaps on the floor, or standing supporting each other. Dame Durdon and Simon are back to back down R. *The Blackbirds end their dance and sink to the floor, wings towards the throne*

The Witch enters L

Witch Sleep on, sleep on, in magic sleep
Dream on, dream on in slumber deep

She takes the crown

The Crown is mine. I've won the day.
So with my Blackbirds I'll away.
Upon my broomstick I must fly
To the Land of Nowhere across the sky.
So sleep you fools. Your day is done.
When you awake, we'll all be gone.

The Witch exits L. *The Blackbirds rise, and, in two groups, circle the throne then exit* L *and* R

There is a silence, broken only by the soft snoring of the sleepers

A loud scream is heard off R *and Lucy runs on, holding her hand before her face. She exits* L, *still screaming*

Everyone except Dame Durdon and Simon awakes

King (*awakening with a start*) What? What? (*He looks around him sleepily*)
Chamberlain (*in horror*) Sire—your Crown. It's *gone!*

There is a shocked reaction from everyone

King (*frantically feeling his head*) I'm ruined. Call out the guards! Help! Help!

The Chamberlain runs off. There is general confusion

Dilly Don't worry, Ferdy. You can always buy another.
Rosemary (*running to him*) Oh Daddy. (*She holds on to him tightly*)

The Chamberlain enters in a fluster

Chamberlain The guards, sire. They're all asleep. I can't waken them.
King Throw a bucket of water over them. I must get the Magic Crown back. (*He sinks his head into his hands with despair*)

Dilly Magic Crown? *Magic* Crown?

Valentine (*to the King*) Don't worry, your Majesty. *I'll* get it back for you.

Rosemary But we don't even know who's *taken* it.

Dilly (*to the Chamberlain*) Did he say *Magic* Crown?

Valentine (*pointing*) Look. A feather near the Throne. (*He picks it up*) It must have been the Blackbirds.

King Find them at once. Arrest them. Do *anything*—but find the Magic Crown.

Dilly (*at the top of her voice*) WHAT MAGIC CROWN?

Everyone stops talking and looks at her

King *My* Magic Crown. The one the Fairy Queen gave to me. Without it I'm *ruined.*

Dilly Oh, don't be silly, Ferdinand. How can you be ruined with all *your* lovely money?

Valentine Without the Magic Crown in his possession, all his money will vanish.

Dilly *Vanish?*

Rosemary The palace will fall into decay.

Dilly (*dazed*) His money will *vanish?*

Flip Our clothes turn to rags.

Flop The food to dust.

Dilly (*unbelievingly*) His money will *vanish?*

King (*jumping up*) I must go to my counting-house at once. Before it's too late. Chamberlain.

Supported by the Chamberlain, the King exits

Dilly That's torn it. I'll never get the palace back from the Abbey National now. (*She begins to exit*)

Valentine Where are you going, Mother?

Dilly To the parlour, of course. I want some bread and honey.

Valentine Bread and honey? Whatever for?

Dilly Well for one thing, it might be the last thing I get to eat for some time, and for another—it's in the rhyme. Toodle-oo.

Dilly exits

Rosemary (*holding Valentine*) Oh, Valentine. What are we going to do? The Magic Crown's gone, and we've no idea where to find it. I'm sure something terrible is going to happen to us now.

There is a great clap of thunder and lightning flashes. All cower in fright

Valentine (*bravely*) Don't be frightened, everyone.

The thunder crashes again

Rosemary The fairy magic that protected us. It's gone. It's the end for us all.

The guests all cry out in terror and exit

Valentine (*calling*) Come back!

The King totters in, clutching a handful of dead leaves

King I'm finished. Finished. I was in my counting-house, counting out my money, and suddenly it all turned into dead leaves. (*He throws a handful into the air*) We're ruined.

The King exits, followed by Flip and Flop. Dilly enters, very distressed

Dilly Oh, help. Help. I'm stricken with ghost-itis. Haunted.
Valentine (*worried*) What's happened?
Dilly I was in the parlour eating my bread and honey—and it *happened*. Right in front of my eyes. The bread turned into a lump of smelly old mould, and the honey—all that thick runny honey—went all down the front of my liberty bodice. (*She mops at her bust*) Oh, and it isn't half sticky.
Valentine Well, I suppose it could have been worse.
Dilly You're right. I could have been wearing a clean one. Oh, Valentine. I'm so hungry I could eat a horse. (*She sobs*)
Rosemary Don't cry, Queen Dilly. I'll go and see if there's anything left in the stables—I mean—*kitchens*.
Dilly Don't bother, love. I'll do it myself. Just tell me where they've set the mousetraps and I'll survive.

Dilly exits

Rosemary Oh, Valentine. We must find the Crown before something even *more* terrible happens.
Valentine I'll begin the search at once. Never fear. It'll be back in your father's hands before the night is out. I'll soon find the Blackbirds' nest.

Fairy Gossamer enters R *in a white light*

Fairy Brave Valentine, Sweet Rosemary;
Hark, I bid, awhile to me.
Your quest I fear will be in vain
Unless you know the culprit's name.
The one you seek is old Witch Watt.
The crown *she* stole. The Blackbirds not.
So to her castle you must hie
In the Land of Nowhere, across the sky.
The way is fraught with cruel danger,
And to her realm you'll be a stranger.
But fear you not. Honest aid you'll find
From those at first who are inclined

To think that *you're* a villain, too.
Though they'll soon learn your heart is true.
Go quickly now. To her castle fly.
And remember too—*I'm* nearby.

Fairy Gossamer exits R

Valentine So, Witch Watt has the Magic Crown, has she? I've heard of her evil doings before. Well this time, she'll find she's met her match.

Rosemary Be careful, Valentine.

Valentine Don't worry, Rosemary. The Crown will be in your father's hands again before you can say Jack Robinson.

Rosemary If only that were true.

Valentine I swear it. Now cheer up. Nothing will stop me regaining it, and the moment I return, I shall ask for your hand in marriage.

SONG TEN

At the end of the song, Valentine and Rosemary exit, arms around each other

For a moment there is silence, then there is a very loud snore from Dame Durdon. Simon wakes with a start

Simon Yes, Dame Durdon. No, Dame Durdon. Sorry, Dame Durdon. I wasn't listening ... (*He realizes*) Oh—I must have been asleep. (*He notices Dame Durdon and shakes her awake*) Chloë. Chloë. Wake up.

Dame (*waking*) Eh? Wazzermarra? Hmmm? Hmm?

Simon (*getting to his feet*) Everybody's gone home. There's nobody left. (*He helps her to her feet*)

Dame I'm not surprised they've all gone. What a boring party. Nothing ever happens here.

The Lights fade to a Black-out and—

the CURTAIN *falls*

SCENE 6

Outside the Royal Palace

Townsfolk hurry across from R *to* L, *dressed in tatters, and wailing. They are followed by the Blackbirds, who perform a short ballet. At the end of the dance they exit after the townsfolk, and the* CURTAIN *rises on—*

SCENE 7

The Haunted Bedroom

In the centre of the room is a large tumbledown double bed, with a rickety dressing-table beside it

Dilly and Dame Durdon enter, holding candles in old-fashioned holders

Dame It's awfully good of you to let me spend the night here with you, Dilly. Especially after all that fuss. I'm really looking forward to a spot of peace and quiet.

Dilly Well if you can't give your own sister a night's lodgings, it's a bit of a bad job, isn't it? You can pay me the four pounds fifty tomorrow morning.

Dame Four pounds fifty? What's that for?

Dilly Well, I can't charge you for breakfast, can I? There's nothing left in the place to eat. (*She puts her candle on the dresser*) I'll just go and put me nighty on.

Dilly exits

Dame Oh, I am looking forward to this. (*She puts her candle on the other side of the dresser*) Lovely soft bed. (*She pats it*) Ouch! They must have stuffed it with concrete.

Her candle is blown out

Oh.

She lights it again with Dilly's candle, puts Dilly's candle down, and that is blown out

That's funny. There must be a draught.

She re-lights Dilly's candle with her own, then, holding her own in her upstage hand, watches Dilly's candle. Her own candle is extinguished

There. That seems to have fixed it. (*She sees her own candle*) Oooer!

Dilly's candle slides slowly to the other end of the dresser then comes to a halt

Dilly—Dilly—DILLYYYYYYYY!

Dilly dashes in, half undressed

Dilly What's the matter?

Dame That candle. It moved.

Dilly Don't be so silly, Chloë. It's an inanimate object.

Dame I don't care what it is. It moved right across that dresser. (*To the audience*) Didn't it, kids?

Dilly Oh, they're as stupid as you are. Of course it didn't move. Now just behave yourself while I go finish getting ready.

Dilly exits

Dame (*looking after her*) It's all right for you. I know what I saw. (*She looks at the candle*) It went right from there to there.

The candle moves back to its original position

Dilly—Dilly—DILLYYYYYYYYY!

Dilly dashes in again

Dilly What is it? What is it?
Dame It's that candle again. The one that didn't move. It hasn't moved again. Right back to where it came from.
Dilly (*firmly*) I don't believe it.
Dame But it's true. They saw it as well, didn't you, kids? (*To Dilly*) See?
Dilly (*sniffing*) I don't care what they saw. Now I'm going to finish getting undressed and I don't want you to call me again. Is that understood?
Dame But what shall I do if it moves again?
Dilly Hit it with something.

Dilly exits

Dame (*nervously*) Hit it with something. Yes. That's what I'll do. (*She picks up her own candlestick and glares at Dilly's*) Right. Go on. I dare you.

Nothing happens. Dame Durdon turns away triumphantly. The candle moves

Dilly enters in her nighty

Dilly Has it moved?
Dame No. It's just where I left it. (*She looks and reacts*) Eeek! Oh ... Dilly. I'm sure this room's haunted.
Dilly Don't be ridiculous. There's no such thing as ghosts. Now go get into your nighty while I get into bed. (*She gets into bed*)
Dame (*putting her candle down*) I'm not going over there on my own. I'll get ready here.
Dilly Oh, all right, then. But hurry up.

Dame Durdon does a big burlesque "strip". At the end of the routine, she scrambles into bed with Dilly

Dame Good night, Dilly. (*She puts her head down*)
Dilly Hey. Did you remember to look under the bed?
Dame (*sitting up*) What for?
Dilly To see if there's a man there, of course.
Dame (*wide-eyed*) What shall we do if there is?
Dilly We give him three weeks to get out.
Dame I'll have a look. (*She gets out of bed and down on her knees to peer under it*) No. There's nothing under here except an old——
Dilly Never mind.
Dame Oh—and it isn't half a big one.
Dilly (*firmly*) It doesn't matter. Forget about it.
Dame There's ever such a pretty pattern round the edges.
Dilly (*more firmly*) I don't want to know about it.
Dame Aren't you going to use it?

Dilly (*loudly*) No, I am *not*!

Dame I am. (*She reaches under the bed and pulls out a large night-cap with a patterned edge. She puts it on*) Isn't it nice? (*She gets back into bed*)

Dilly What about the candle? Aren't you going to blow it out?

Dame Oh, I haven't to get out of bed again, have I?

Voice Allow me.

The candle is blown out

Dame Thank you. (*She realizes*) Oooer!

Dilly (*clutching her*) I don't think I like this room after all.

Dame Me neither. Let's try to get some sleep. The kids'll warn us if anything comes in while we're not looking, won't you? Now don't forget. Nighty-night.

Dame Durdon and Dilly settle down. As they do so, a huge hairy spider drops from above them and hovers. When the audience "warns them", Dame Durdon sits up

What is it? Who's there? (*She looks around*) What? A *glider*? In here? Don't be silly. It'd never get its wings in. Oh . . . A spider. Where?

The spider vanishes upwards again

I can't see one. (*She looks around and up and down*) Oh, you're having me on, aren't you? You're not? Honest? Oh, well I'd better get out of bed and have a proper look. (*She gets out*) Over here, was it? Above me? (*She looks above her*) I can't see it. (*She moves away from the bed and the spider drops to just above Dilly's face*) Over here? (*She moves down front and keeps her back to Dilly*)

Dilly (*wakening*) Who are you talking to, Chloë?

Dame (*without turning*) They say there's a spider in here.

Dilly Oh, never mind about a spider. Get back into bed. I'm freezing.

Dame But it might be lurking.

Dilly I don't care what it's doing. Get back into bed. (*Without looking, she reaches out, grabs the spider and pulls it into the bed with her*) Now go to sleep.

Dame (*turning*) Well give me a chance to get in.

Dame Durdon moves to the bed. The spider rises into the air. She screams. Dilly jumps up and leaps out of bed. There is a panic as the spider vanishes

Dilly (*recovering*) Oh, Chloë.

Dame (*gasping*) Oh, Dilly.

Dilly I'll never sleep again.

Dame Me neither.

Witch Watt scuttles in L, *in a green light*

Shrieking with laughter, the Witch signals off

Ghosts, skeletons, rats, etc., tumble on

Dame Durdon and Dilly jump on to the bed. The spider drops on to them and the bed collapses, as—

the CURTAIN *falls*

ACT II

Scene 1

The Courtyard of the Palace

When the Curtain *rises, the courtyard is filled with townsfolk in shabby clothing. Valentine, sword by his side, is addressing them*

Valentine The Magic Crown will soon be restored to its rightful owner, and if all goes well, the Witch will perish and I shall return to claim the hand of the Princess Rosemary. But now for the business at hand. What the Witch has done with sorcery, I shall do with the aid of my sword. So come, give me a song to cheer me on my way.

SONG ELEVEN

At the end of the song, Valentine exits L

The Townsfolk gather in little groups and chat (silently) to one another

Rosemary, in shabby clothing, enters R

Rosemary It's no use. I can't let him search for the Witch alone. I've got to follow him. (*She looks around*) My poor people. Clothing turning to rags, and no food to eat. We've just *got* to get the Crown back. (*Calling*) Valentine. Wait!

Rosemary hurries off L. *As she does so, King Ferdinand, in ragged robes, and Queen Dilly, in a new costume, enter* R

Dilly —and I know *just* the place to pawn the crown jewels.
King (*weakly*) I keep telling you, there's no crown jewels left. They've all gone. Vanished.
Dilly But they can't have done. *Mine* haven't.
King You don't live in Cornucopia. The curse only applies to us.
Dilly Well, surely you've got something tucked away under your mattress? A tattered tiara? A dented diamond? A ruptured ruby?
King (*loudly*) No, no, no. Nothing. Not even a brass farthing. I'm ruined.
Dilly (*annoyed*) How dare you be ruined? I always knew you were sly, Ferdinand. You've done this to *spite* me, haven't you? Arranged all this just to spoil my visit.
King To spoil your visit? (*Angrily*) This is all *your* fault, you interfering old busybody. If you hadn't opened that pie, then none of this would have happened.
Dilly And whose *birthday* was it, eh? (*She prods him*) *Yours.* If anybody is to blame it's *you.* (*She prods him again*)

King (*backing away*) Dilly . . .

Dilly (*following*) You should be persecuted by the police for leaving dangerous things like that pie standing around. Thank goodness I found out about you in time to stop the wedding.

King (*startled*) Wedding? What wedding?

Dilly Rosemary and Valentine's, of course. (*She turns away*) Oh, when I think how you nearly tricked me into letting my son marry your daughter.

King But—but . . .

Dilly Don't try to deny it. Anyway, your little trick hasn't worked. We're leaving for Utopia in the morning.

The Chamberlain, Flip and Flop enter all in shabby outfits

Chamberlain (*excitedly*) Sire. Oh, sire. It's the Princess. She's vanished.

King Vanished? Are you sure?

Flip We've searched the entire palace.

Flop And the grounds.

Dilly (*almost swooning with delight*) Oh, how romantic. They've run off together.

King Who have?

Dilly Rosemary and Valentine. They've enveloped to get married.

Chamberlain Oh, no, your Majesty. The young Prince left the palace some time ago.

King (*horror-struck*) Then—then she must have been kidnapped. (*He wails*) Oh, Rosemaryyyy.

Dilly (*singing*) "I love you. I'm always thinking of you."

King (*shouting*) Silence, woman! This is an emergency. My only daughter has been kidnapped. She's got to be rescued. Chamberlain. Make a proclamation. Whoever finds my daughter will be richly rewarded.

Dilly Here, I say . . .

King Shut up.

Dilly But . . .

King (*loudly*) SILENCE! (*To the Chamberlain*) Well, get on with it.

Chamberlain Oyez, oyez, oyez!

The townsfolk all take notice and move in

Let it be known that the Princess Rosemary has been kidnapped, and a rich reward will be given to whoever shall find her.

Boy Who's going to pay the reward?

King I am, of course.

Girl What with? Dead leaves?

Dilly (*to the King*) That's what I was trying to tell you.

King (*snapping*) You keep quiet. (*To the townsfolk*) I'll give a knighthood to the one who finds my daughter.

Boy What's the good of a knighthood in a bankrupt country?

King (*in despair*) I'll give *anything*.

The townsfolk jeer and exit

Wait! Come back! (*He groans*) Oh, it's hopeless.

Flip (*disgustedly*) With friends like them, who needs enemies?

Flop What a rotten lot. Not *one* of 'em willing to help find the Princess. (*He calls*) Cowards!

King You're right. They're all afraid. But we're not beaten yet. (*To the Jesters*) *You* can go and find her.

Flip
Flop } (*Speaking together*) Us?

King Yes. And if you dare come back without her ... (*He draws his finger across his throat*)

Flip and Flop tremble

The King, the Chamberlain and Dilly exit R

Flip That's torn it. I can't stand the sight of blood.

Flop Don't worry. You won't be around to see it. Oh, what are we going to do?

Flip Start looking. (*He hurries around the courtyard*)

Flop What are you *doing*?

Flip Looking for Rosemary.

Flop Well you won't find her here, you fool. If you ask me, she's gone after that Prince Turpentine—to the Witch's Lair.

Flip Oh. The Witch's Lair. (*He laughs weakly*) Well, in that case, we needn't bother to go looking for her, need we?

Flop You're not *scared*, are you?

Flip Who, *me*? Of course I'm not scared. My family motto is "No Fear".

Flop "No Fear". That's a very good motto. How did you get it?

Flip Well, every time somebody wanted one of us to do something dangerous, we all said "No Fear".

Flop I might have guessed. Anyway, there's nothing to be afraid of. All you've got to do is sneak into the Witch's Lair, tell Rosemary that her dad's looking for her, then come back here and we can collect the reward. It's dead simple.

Flip What do you mean, all *I* have to do? What about you? What are *you* to do?

Flop What do you *think* I'm going to do, stupid? I'm going to wait here and run for help if the Witch catches you.

Flip What's the good of that? The Witch's Lair is miles away.

Flop (*with great patience*) I know it is, numbskull. That's why I shall be waiting here. If the Witch *does* catch you, then I shan't have so far to run to get help, will I?

Flip Oh—I never thought of that.

Flop Of course you didn't. You never think about anything, do you? Now hurry up and get going before it gets dark.

Flip Why is it that *I* have to do all the dirty work? Why can't I stay here and wait, and run for help if *you* get captured?

Flop Because it was my idea, that's why. Now stop complaining and get going.
Flip No.
Flop I'm warning you. If you're not out of my sight in two minutes, I'll . . .
Flip You'll what?
Flop I'll punch you right on the nose.
Flip (*sneering*) Ha—you and whose army? You couldn't knock the skin off a rice pudding.
Flop (*waving his fists*) Is that so?

SONG TWELVE

After the song, Flip and Flop exit L, *arguing furiously. As they do so, Dame Durdon and Simon enter* R *shabbily dressed*

Dame (*wailing*) Oh, Simon. Whatever are we going to do? Everything's crumbling to dust, and poor Rosemary's missicating. Kidnapped by the Gypsies from under our very noses while everybody had their backs turned. (*She sniffles*)
Simon Don't cry, Chloë. We'll soon have everything put right again. All we've got to do is go after that Prince Valentine and tell him what's happened, then while he's looking for Rosemary, we can carry on to the Witch's Lair and get the Magic Crown back.
Dame Us?
Simon Why not? We might even get a reward from King Ferdinand. Once he's got the Crown back, he'll have all his money again.
Dame You're right.
Simon Then when everything's back to normal, I'm going to ask for a certain someone's hand in marriage.
Dame (*fluttering*) Oh, Simon. Are you really?
Simon I certainly am.
Dame Someone young and attractive? (*She preens herself*)
Simon Oh, yes.
Dame Winsome and cuddly?
Simon Oh, *yes*.
Dame Gentle and lovable?
Simon Oh, *yes*.
Dame Is it *me*?
Simon No. It's Lucy the maid.
Dame What? (*She grabs him*)
Simon (*quickly*) I was only kidding, Chloë. Of course it's you. Lucy's all right, but it's you I really fancy. Every time I look at you I think I'm in heaven.
Dame (*releasing him*) Oh, Simon. Every time you look at me you think you're in heaven. Is that because I remind you of an angel?
Simon You certainly do. (*Aside*) You're like nothing on earth.
Dame (*suspiciously*) What was that?
Simon Nothing . . . (*He smiles sweetly at her*)
Dame Oh, Simon. Just imagine. Married after all these years. But you'll

have to propose to me properly, you know. Somewhere where there's sweet music and dim, dim lights. (*She flutters*)

Simon (*looking at her face*) I think I'd prefer the lights to be out altogether.

Dame And we'll sit on the sofa in front of the fire, and you can get a little bolder—and I can get a little bolder . . .

Simon Are we going to build a rockery?

Dame Then you can gaze into my eyes and tell me how beautiful they are.

Simon And how they remind me of mountain pools.

Dame Deep, Silent and Mysterious?

Simon No. Covered in pondweed.

Dame And then you can take me in your arms and cover me with kisses.

Simon I'd sooner cover you with a thick blanket.

Dame (*clutching at her bosom*) You don't seem to realize what lies here—waiting for you.

Simon Yes, I do. Two and a half pounds of cotton wool.

Dame (*sobbing*) Ooooooh! I'm cut to the quick.

Simon Oh, don't cry, Chloë. I was only joking.

Dame Well I'm fed up with you trifling with my confections. You can go and marry your rotten old Lucy. I'll go and look for Rosemary on my own. (*She begins to exit, sniffling*)

Simon Hey—come back, Chloë. I didn't mean it, honest. I don't really want to marry Lucy. Come on. Smile for Simon.

Dame Shan't.

Simon Oh, go on.

Dame No.

Simon Force yourself.

Dame Well—coax me, then.

SONG THIRTEEN

At the end of the song Dame Durdon and Simon exit R. *Witch Watt enters* L, *in a green light, and watches them go*

Witch Go seek, you fools. You'll never find.
The Magic Crown I claim as mine.
But—where can the Princess be?
And Valentine? It cannot be
That they know where the Crown lies hid?
But if so, I my demons bid
To keep it safe from prying eyes
Whilst I prepare a new surprise.
Then when they enter to my room
They'll also enter to their *doom*.

She cackles with laughter

Fairy Gossamer enters R *in a white light*

Fairy One moment, friend, you go too fast.

You'll find your plan will fail.
For once again, as in the past,
True goodness will prevail.
Return to me the Magic Crown
And I promise you shall live.
If not—then Valentine I'll aid
And the fatal blow, *he'll* give.

Witch (*snarling*) I've warned you once. I'll warn you twice.
Hear this—and understand.
Try but once more to interfere
And there'll be one less fairy in Fairyland.

Fairy You can't harm me, you Ancient hag.
Your hour is almost past.

Witch Just cross my path again, my *dear*—
And I swear 'twill be the last.

Fairy So be it then. The die is cast;
Our battle must begin.
Farewell until we meet again—
And may the best one win.

Fairy Gossamer exits R

Witch (*shouting*) Don't worry. I *will*!

The Witch laughs and exits L, *as*—

the CURTAIN *falls*

SCENE 2

A Woodland Path
Babes, dressed as rabbits, enter and perform a dance to SONG FOURTEEN.
As it finishes, the CURTAIN *rises on*—

SCENE 3

The Gypsy Encampment

A very colourful scene, set amongst trees. To one side is a fire, and an old Gypsy Woman is beside it, stirring a cauldron. Several Gypsies stand around, watching others perform a fiery dance. At the end of the number, all shout

Zorika, the attractive sweetheart of the Lord of the Gypsies, enters R

Zorika (*moving to the old woman*) No sign of Rollo, yet?
Woman Not yet, Zorika. The moon has only just risen.
Zorika The camp seems so lonely without him.
Woman He'll return shortly. I can see the signs in the fire.

Zorika (*crouching beside her*) Oh, Meg. You're so old and wise. Tell me my fortune.

Woman Give me your palm, little one. (*She takes Zorika's hand and peers at it*) I see—I see a dark young man—very handsome.

Rollo, Lord of the Gypsies enters R

He seems to be looking for someone.

Rollo tiptoes down behind Zorika

He is about to speak.

Zorika (*eagerly*) What does he say?

Rollo (*loudly*) Boo!

Zorika leaps up with a squeal. Everyone laughs

Zorika Rollo.

Zorika and Rollo embrace

Rollo So—my little Zorika was worried about me, was she?

Zorika (*breaking free*) Certainly not. But if the Witch had caught you . . .

Rollo (*laughing*) Don't worry about her. I'm not afraid of that cackling old hag any longer. And besides—why should I care about her? You're the only witch I'll ever dream about. The witch who has captured my heart in a net of stars, and bound me to her forever.

SONG FIFTEEN

At the end of the song, two Gypsies enter L *holding Valentine between them—a prisoner. Squint, a very small Gypsy, is with them*

Rollo Hello—and what have we here?

Gypsy It's a spy. We found him in the woods.

Squint (*drawing a huge knife*) Let me kill him.

Valentine I'm *not* a spy. I am Prince Valentine of Utopia, and I'm looking for the Lair of Witch Watt, so I can regain the Magic Crown of King Ferdinand which she has stolen from him.

There is a murmur from the Gypsies

Zorika How do we know if he's speaking the truth? This could be a trap to capture us.

Squint (*waving his knife*) Let me kill him.

Rollo No. We must think. This *may* be a trap . . . but on the other hand, he *could* be telling the truth. Take him to the cave and guard him whilst we find out if the Crown has indeed been stolen.

Squint (*pleading*) Please let me kill him.

Rollo Take him away.

They begin to drag Valentine off

Rosemary is pulled on by two more Gypsies

Rosemary Let me go! Let me go! (*She sees Valentine*) Valentine! (*She breaks free and runs to him*)
Valentine Rosemary! What are *you* doing here?
Rollo (*dropping on one knee*) Rosemary. Your Highness.
Zorika (*sinking to the floor in a deep curtsy*) Princess.

All the Gypsies kneel

Rosemary (*surprised*) Rollo. Zorika. *You!*
Valentine (*startled*) You know them?
Rosemary Of course I do. Rollo was a footman at the palace and Zorika was a serving-maid. One day they were dismissed for stealing gold from the treasury, a few coins at a time so that they would not be missed. I *knew* it couldn't be true, so in my disguise as a peasant girl I kept watch —and saw the real culprit. A jackdaw. But by that time Rollo and Zorika had fled the country. We've been searching for them ever since to beg their forgiveness. (*She holds out her hands to them*)
Rollo And we give it gladly. (*He springs to his feet*)
Rosemary Then you'll return to the palace with us?
Zorika Of course. (*She rises*) But what about our gallant band of outlaws? What is to become of *them*?
Valentine When the Witch is dead, her Castle and lands shall be given to them so that they can begin to lead an honest life once more.
Squint An honest life? (*He groans*) Why didn't you let me kill him?

All laugh

Rollo Then let us celebrate, for we have food and wine in plenty, and the violins will play sweet tonight.
Valentine No. There'll be plenty of time for celebrations when the Witch is dead, but right now I must head for her Lair.
Rosemary You mean we. I'm coming with you.
Rollo No, your Highness. The Witch's Lair is no place for a girl.
Zorika Rollo is right. Evil things happen there.
Rosemary But no harm will come to me if Valentine is there. And besides, the Fairy promised she'd be near at hand.
Valentine (*to Rosemary*) You're right. I'm sure there'll be no danger.
Rollo Then I'll send some of my men to escort you there.
Valentine Many thanks. I'll see that they are suitably rewarded. Farewell.

Valentine, Rosemary and some Gypsies exit R

Rollo (*to the others*) Well, don't just stand there looking at one another. We have work to do.

Everyone exits in haste. When the set is empty, Flip and Flop enter L

Flip (*looking around*) I wonder where we are?
Flop The middle of the second act. That's where we are. The Gypsy Encampment. Didn't you buy a programme? It's got your name in it.

Flip Gypsy Encampment? Quick. Let's get out of here before they start trying to sell us some clothes pegs.
Flop (*looking off*) Too late. Somebody's coming.

Rollo enters with Squint and another Gypsy

Rollo Aha. And who do we have here?

The Gypsies draw their knives

Jesters (*clutching each other in fright*) Oooer!
Rollo Who are you? (*He gestures at them with the knife*)
Flop We—we . . .
Rollo Ah, Frenchmen?
Flip No. We're jesters.
Rollo Jesters, eh? And what are your names?
Flop He's Flip, and I'm Flop.
Rollo Unusual names. How did you get them?
Flip Well we've both got a shoe with a split sole, and when we walk side by side, they go flip, flop, flip, flop, flip, flop.

Flip and Flop laugh but the others do not

Squint Let me kill 'em.
Rollo What are you doing in my camp?
Flop Looking.
Rollo Looking for what?
Flip The lost chord.

Flip and Flop laugh

Rollo I'll put a cord round your necks in a minute.
Squint Please let me kill 'em. (*He prods Flip and Flop with his knife*)
Rollo Now for the last time—what do you want?
Flop A pint of bitter, please.
Flip And a glass of Harpic with a cherry in it.
Rollo (*shouting*) What are you doing here?
Flop Naughty, naughty. You said you'd asked us for the last time.
Rollo (*almost screeching*) Are you FOOLS?
Flip Of course we are. Why do you think we're dressed like this?
Rollo (*furiously*) This is impossible. Take them away before I go mad.
Squint Let me kill 'em. (*He stabs Flip's posterior with his knife*)
Flip Yee-owww! Call him off!

Squint repeats his action with Flop, and they both dash off chased by Squint and the other Gypsy. As they exit, Dame Durdon and Simon are brought on by more Gypsies

Dame (*struggling*) Help, put me down! You don't know where I've been.
Rollo (*turning in disbelief*) Another pair?
Gypsy We found them gallivanting in the shrubbery.

Dame How dare you. I haven't vanted my galli in all my life.

Rollo Who are you, my good woman?

Dame I'm not your good woman. I'm nobody's good woman. And if this little squirt doesn't let go of me, I'll flatten him.

The Gypsy hurriedly lets go of Dame Durdon

Rollo What do you want?

Dame What do I want? What do I want? He drags me here under false pretendrances and then he asks me what I want. (*Very fiercely*) I'll tell you what I want . . .

Rollo (*loudly*) Silence, you old faggot!

Simon Here. Don't you call the old faggot an old faggot.

Rollo (*to Simon*) Shut up!

Simon Don't you tell me to shut up. (*He rears to his full height*)

Rollo also rears to his full height, and Simon hides behind Dame Durdon

Dame Durdon's not frightened of *you*.

Rollo Take them to the cave.

Dame Lay one finger on me, and I'll scream the place down.

Zorika and Squint enter

Zorika (*seeing them*) *More* of them?

Squint (*drawing his knife*) Let me kill 'em.

Dame (*to Squint*) Listen, Jack the Zipper. If you don't stop waving that pencil sharpener about—I'll FILLET you with it!

Squint (*bursting into tears with shock*) Awwwwwww!

Zorika (*comforting him*) Now look what you've done.

Simon She never laid a finger on the little worm.

Rollo Silence, you brainless dolt.

Dame Here—don't you mock the affiliated.

Rollo Get them out of here. They're driving me mad.

The Gypsies advance on them

Dame Help. Fire. Police.

Simon Keep back—or I'll do something desperate.

The Gypsies keep advancing

I'm warning you. If you come one step further—I'll blow you all to pieces. (*He raises his hand to shoulder height*)

Witch Watt enters behind Simon and Dame Durdon, and can only be seen by the Gypsies

Rollo (*spotting the Witch*) Come back. Quickly.

The Gypsies retreat

Simon (*advancing*) Aha. That's scared you, hasn't it? All I've got to do is drop my hand like this—(*He pretends to drop his hand*)—and you'll go up in smoke.

The Witch moves forward behind Dame Durdon and Simon. The Gypsies back away in horror

Now who's the boss, eh? (*He pretends to drop his hand several times*) Drop. Drop. Drop.

The Witch raises her hands

The Gypsies turn and flee in terror

Aha! They've gone.

Dame Oh, Simon, you were wonderful.

Simon (*with much false modesty*) Oh, it was nothing.

Dame Nothing? You just saved our lives. And as an extra special reward, you can give me a great big kiss. (*She puckers her lips*)

Simon All right. (*He turns to face her and spots the Witch*) Oooer!

Dame Well, come on then. Get on with it. My lips are getting chapped.

Simon Ah—ah—ah . . . (*He tries to indicate the Witch behind her*)

Dame What's the matter? Can't you get your breath?

Simon tries to speak, but can only make strangled noises. His finger jabs at the Witch

What are you doing? Pressing buttons? Do you want to go up in a lift?

Simon screws up his face and shakes his head. Dame Durdon turns in bafflement and sees the Witch behind her

Oh—is *that* what all the fuss is about?

Witch (*cackling*) He he he.

Dame (*going up to her*) Just the woman I've been looking for. What about my money for baking that pie?

Witch Money?

Dame Yes, money. Cash. Dough. Bread. Chinky-chinky.

Witch (*snarling*) You'll get no money from me.

Dame Oh, won't I? We'll see about that. (*She snatches the Witch's broomstick*) Now do I get that money, or am I going to wrap this sweeping-brush round your earhole?

Witch (*snatching the broom back*) Take your hands off my broom.

Dame Oh! You want to fight, do you? Right. (*She dashes into the wings and rushes back on with a "stick"*) Take *that*. (*She lashes out at the Witch*)

The Witch screams in fright and dashes off in a hurry

Simon (*staring at Dame Durdon in wonderment*) Gosh, Chloë. I never realized you were so brave.

Dame (*twirling the "stick"*) Anybody could have got rid of *her*.

Simon Yes. But not by hitting her with a *rattlesnake*.

Dame Durdon looks at the "stick", realizes, and throws it away from her with a shriek. She faints into Simon's arms as—

the CURTAIN *falls*

SCENE 4

A Quiet Glade

The King rushes on, pursued by Dilly

King Will you please shut up and leave me alone?

Dilly But it's a wonderful idea, Ferdinand. If you marry me, you can claim National Assistance for both of us, and we can live in my palace in Utopia—with a bit of luck.

King But I don't want to live in Utopia. And I most certainly don't want to marry you.

Dilly Of course you do. Kiss me (*She advances on him*)

King (*retreating*) Keep away.

Dilly Oh, don't be shy.

King I'm not shy. I'm worried.

Dilly Worried? What about?

King About everything. Rosemary. My Magic Crown. Poor little Lucy's nose . . .

Dilly Oh, you don't have to worry about Lucy's nose. That pretty little fairy creature stuck it back on again for her—and as for Rosemary and the Crown—somebody's *bound* to find them.

King Well, I hope so, because if they don't, I'm going to ask you to . . .

Dilly Marry you? (*She swoons*) I knew it.

King To leave my kingdom at once. You've caused more chaos since you arrived, than a bull in a china shop.

Dilly Oh, you say the nicest things, Ferdinand. Kiss me, kiss me, kiss me.

King Control yourself, woman.

Dilly (*wagging her finger at him*) That's the best of being a woman. She doesn't *have* to control herself.

SONG SIXTEEN

The King flies for his life

Oh well. I wasn't trained in hunting for nothing. (*She shouts*) Yoicks! Tally ho!

Dilly exits after the King as the CURTAIN *rises on—*

Scene 5

The Witch's Lair

The room is dark and gloomy, with a throne at the back, on which the Witch sits surrounded by her minions (or the Blackbirds)

Witch The day is done, the hour is nigh,
And very soon the Prince must die.
The fairy said *he'd* vanquish *me*.
Ha ha—I know 'twill never be.
What chance has he against my spell?
What can he do? No one can tell.
(*Standing in a fury*) I'll teach them not to threaten me.
To fear the words I say. (*She darts a quick glance off*)
But hush—footsteps I hear outside.
The Prince doth come this way.

She signals, and her minions rise and melt into the shadows. She hides behind the throne

Valentine enters with Rosemary

Valentine What a gloomy place this is. Fitting indeed for someone as evil as the Witch.
Rosemary (*looking around*) I wonder where she is?
Valentine Engaged on some dirty work, I'll be bound. But we have no time to lose. We must find out where the Magic Crown is hidden. You search in here, and I'll look around the other rooms.

Valentine exits R

Rosemary begins to look around. As she does so, the Witch creeps out from behind the throne and tiptoes down behind her

Dame (*off*) Coo-ee. Anybody home?

The Witch quickly scuttles behind the throne again

Dame Durdon enters in a fantastic Gypsy costume

Rosemary (*surprised*) Dame Durdon? What on earth are *you* doing here?
Dame (*embracing her*) Oh, Rosemary. Thank goodness you're safe. We thought you'd been kidnapped.
Rosemary And you came looking for me? All on your own?
Dame Well—not exactly. I brought Simon along for company.
Rosemary Where is he?
Dame He'll be along in a minute. He's having trouble getting up the stairs. He has to carry the doublets, you see.
Rosemary But doublets aren't heavy, Dame Durdon.
Dame Oh, these are. Flip and Flop are still inside 'em.
Rosemary You mean they came along, too? Oh, how brave of you all.

Simon, Flip and Flop enter

Simon Princess.

They all embrace

Rosemary (*after the greetings are over*) I must tell Valentine you're here. He's in the next room.

Rosemary exits

Simon I wonder if he's had any luck finding the Crown?
Dame I don't know, but if we don't get a bit more light in here, we're not going to find anything.
Flip Let's make a fire. That'll give us some light.
Flop Good idea. It'll warm the place up too. I'm freezing.
Simon (*looking around*) What are we going to burn?
Dame Well, there's that rickety old bath-chair over there. (*She points to the throne*) That'll do.
Flip We'll get it.

Flip and Flop pick up the throne and carry it down to the others. Witch Watt is revealed crouching behind nothing

Simon (*pointing*) The Witch!
Flop And she's got the Crown.
Dame Quick, Simon. Surround her!
Witch (*rearing up*) Stay back, or by my demon hordes
Your lives will soon be ended.
This Magic Crown is mine alone.
For me it was intended.
Dame You nasty rotten thieving Witch.
That's Ferdy's Crown you stole.
So give it back, or else I'll clout you
Round the flipping earhole.
Oh, crikey. She's got me at it now. (*To the Witch*) Come on.
Hand it over. (*She advances on her*)
Witch No, no. (*She backs away*) The Crown is mine. All mine.
And whilst I still draw breath,
Will stay mine—and to guard it
My four black Knights of death . . . (*She points*)

Four men in black holding swords enter. They wear masks

Simon Oh, heck. Manchester United supporters.

Flip and Flop try to hide behind each other

Dame (*calling*) Valentine! Help! Help!

Valentine and Rosemary enter

Valentine What is it? (*He sees the Knights*)
Witch Kill them.
Valentine Just let me see you try it. (*He draws his sword*)

The four Knights rush at Valentine. Rosemary drops back. A sword fight begins. The Witch circles the fighters, urging on her demons. Valentine kills them one by one. When the last is dead, he turns to face her

And now to settle with *you.*

The Witch recoils in terror and bumps into Simon who grabs the Crown from her head

The Witch exits with a shriek of rage

Dame (*loudly*) We've got the Crown! We've got the Crown!

All congratulate Valentine and one another

Valentine And now to return to the palace, and hand the Crown back to its rightful owner.
Rosemary *And* claim the reward. (*She holds out her hand with a smile*)
Flip But what about the Witch?
Flop She might come back and put a horrible curse on us!
Valentine (*laughing*) We've nothing more to fear from her. She'll be miles away by now. We'll never set eyes on her again.
Rosemary We must let Rollo know the good news at once. I'll see if the two men who brought us here are still waiting outside.

Rosemary exits

Valentine And we'll load up all the treasure I've found in the next room. It must be everything the Witch ever stole in her life. Come on.
Simon Oh, Chloë. There's bound to be a reward for returning it all, isn't there? We might get enough to buy ourselves a great big house without a bathroom in it.
Dame What do we want one of them for?
Simon So we can be filthy rich.

Flip and Flop take off their hats and hit him with them

All exit into the next room, laughing

Rosemary (*off*) They don't seem to be there, Valentine.

Rosemary enters

I think they must have . . . (*She sees the room is empty*) Oh. (*Looking around*) Valentine? Dame Durdon? Where are you?

Witch Watt creeps in behind Rosemary and seizes her

Help! Help! Valentine!

Struggling helplessly, Rosemary is dragged off. Valentine and the others hurry in

Valentine (*alarmed*) Rosemary! Where are you?
Rosemary (*off*) Help!

There is a cackle of triumph from the Witch

Dame (*horrified*) It's the Witch.
Simon She's captured Rosemary.
Valentine Quickly. After them.

Before they can move, the Blackbirds enter and flutter round them, barring their way to the exit

(*Desperately*) Let me through. Let me through!

There is general confusion, then the Blackbirds fly off. Valentine rushes for the door and exits

Dame Durdon, Simon, Flip and Flop, begin to recover

Flip That's torn it.
Flop Now we really *have* lost her.
Dame Not yet, we haven't. Valentine'll catch them.
Simon Oh, I hope so. You know what'll happen if he doesn't?
Flip (*clutching at his throat*) Oooer. We'll all get our heads chopped off.
Flop And I'm quite attached to mine.
Dame (*looking off*) He's coming back.

Valentine enters, dejectedly

Valentine It's no use. They've gone. Vanished into thin air.

All look at one another in dismay as—

the CURTAIN *falls*

SCENE 6

A Road through the Mountains

The Chamberlain enters L, *Lucy* R

Chamberlain Ah, Lucy. Just the girl I want.
Lucy Sorry. I'm already spoken for.
Chamberlain No, no. I'm looking for the King's whereabouts.
Lucy Well don't look at me. They weren't in the wash this week.
Chamberlain You misunderstand me, Lucy. I am merely seeking cor-

roboration of my assumption, that his Majesty is secretly sojourning in solitudinous solemnity within the immediate proximity of this deserted and desolate panoramic plateau.

Lucy (*blankly*) You what?

Chamberlain (*giving a deep sigh*) 'As 'is Nibs trolled past 'ere, lately?

Lucy Oh. Well why didn't you say so at first? No, love. Haven't seen him.

Chamberlain (*on his dignity*) Don't you "love" me.

Lucy Course I don't. You're not my type.

Chamberlain (*grandly*) I would remind you, young lady, that you are speaking to a gentleman. *I* have blue blood in my veins.

Lucy (*wide-eyed*) Have you? What happened? Did you sit on a fountain-pen, or something?

Chamberlain (*snorting*) Oh, out of my way. (*He begins to exit* R)

Lucy (*laughing*) Here, come back, Mr Chamberlain. I was only teasing you.

Chamberlain (*frostily*) I am not in the habit of allowing the lower classes to tease me, young lady. After all, I *am* the Court Chamberlain.

Lucy (*wrinkling her nose at him*) Oh, go on. You can take a joke, can't you?

Chamberlain (*mellowing*) After eighteen years of working for King Ferdinand, I can take almost anything.

Lucy Eighteen years? Oh, what a smashing time you must have had. 'Ere, I bet you can remember when he first met that Queen Dilly, can't you?

Chamberlain (*trying to appear modest*) Well . . .

Lucy (*eagerly*) How did it happen?

Chamberlain He just opened his wallet, and there she was.

Lucy (*laughing*) Here, you know. You're quite nice, really, aren't you?

Chamberlain I have my admirers.

Lucy Do you think I'll ever get to be a Lady-in-Waiting? I've always dreamed about being one of them. You know. Looking after the Princess.

Chamberlain Well—I don't see why not. You—er—you *do* have a certain attraction, you know.

Lucy (*eagerly*) Have I? (*Downcast*) Oh, go on. (*Shyly*) Do you mean it? Honest?

Chamberlain Of course I do. In fact—*I* wouldn't mind being a *Gentleman* in Waiting—if I were waiting on *you.*

Lucy (*delighted*) Oh, you saucy old thing.

SONG SEVENTEEN

At the end of the song, Lucy and the Chamberlain exit happily R. *As they do so, the scene darkens, and Witch Watt enters* L, *pulling Rosemary behind her*

Rosemary (*struggling*) Let me go! Let me go!

Witch (*snarling*) Silence, girl. Your fate is sealed.
Your life is in my hand.
Sealed inside the living rock
Forever you will stand.

Bound there by a magic spell
Unable to break free
Until the day that . . . Nay, but nay.
That time shall *never* be!

Rosemary (*horrified*) Oh, no. No! Please let me go!

Witch You know full well the Magic Crown
Should rightfully be mine.
For years I've dreamed, for years I've schemed;
To make your star decline.
Yet now I've been outwitted by a stripling fool in love.
I've lost my Crown—but *he*'s lost *you*—
And *I*'ll make the final move.

The Witch drags Rosemary off as she calls for help

Valentine (*off*) Rosemary. Rosemary?

Valentine enters L, *carrying the Crown*

The Lights brighten

Valentine I thought I heard her voice. (*He listens*) No, I must have been mistaken. (*In despair*) Oh, where can she be? I can't go back to the King without her. I have the Magic Crown, but what good is that if Rosemary is missing? (*He realizes*) The Magic Crown. Of course. (*He holds it up*) By the power of this Magic Crown, I call upon the Fairy Gossamer to help me.

Fairy Gossamer enters R *in a white light*

Fairy I hear your voice, brave Valentine.
Fear not. I vow you'll be in time
To catch the Witch and foil her plan.
So hurry, quickly as you can
To the Rock of Eternity, cold and bare.
The Witch *and* Rosemary you'll find there.
And near the spot where the Rock stands grim,
Will be fought the *last* battle
Make sure that you *win*.

Fairy Gossamer exits R

Valentine (*delighted*) Don't worry. I'll win all right. To the rescue.

Dame Durdon and Simon wearily enter L

Quickly. To the Rock of Eternity!

Valentine exits R

Simon (*blankly*) Rock of Eternity? What does he want to go there for?
Dame It's as deserted as a cinema when they play the National Anthem.
Simon Well, I suppose he knows what he's doing. We'd better follow him.
Dame What about Flip and Flop? What's happened to them?
Simon I don't know. I think we lost 'em just after we left the Witch's Lair. We'd better give them a shout.
Dame I'll do it. (*Calling*) Hello-o!
Voice (*off*) Hello-o!

Dame Durdon reacts with surprise

Simon Hey! It's an echo.
Dame Are they dangerous?
Simon No, no. An echo's something that always answers you back.
Dame Oh, I see. It's like you, is it?
Simon Eh?
Dame (*louder*) I said like you.
Voice (*off*) Like you.
Dame No. Like him.
Voice (*off*) Oh, sorry.
Simon (*surprised*) That's funny. (*To Dame Durdon*) Have another go.
Dame You mean try again? (*She thinks then calls*) How are you?
Voice (*off*) Are you?
Dame Am I what?
Voice (*off*) Are you calling to me?
Dame Of course I am, you silly . . . (*She realizes*) Oooer.
Simon (*puzzled*) It shouldn't do that. Let me try. (*Calling*) Mr Echo.
Voice (*off*) Echo.
Simon (*calling*) I'm Simple Simon.
Voice (*off*) And you sound it.
Simon That's no echo. It's somebody playing a trick on us.
Dame I bet it's them two jesters. Messing about when we're supposed to be looking for Rosemary. Just wait till I get my hands on 'em. I'll separate their breath from their bodies.

Flip and Flop enter behind them

Flip Separate whose breath from their bodies?
Dame (*turning to look at them*) Flip and Flop, of course. I'll . . . (*She realizes*) Here. What are you doing out here? You're supposed to be over there trying to make fools of us.
Flop Well, we aren't. Besides, we couldn't improve on nature, could we?
Simon Well, if it's not you over there, who is it? (*He marches over to the far side of the stage and peers off*)

A ghost enters wailing loudly, dashes past them all and exits at the other side

Flip Oooer. It must be haunted round here.

Simon Don't be daft. There's no such thing as ghosts.

Dame Don't you mock at the supernational. There are ghosts in every public house in the country.

Flop Yes. They're Inn-spectres.

Flip Well, I want to go home.

Simon And get your head chopped off for letting the Witch capture Rosemary? Oh, well—if that's what you *want*. But me and Chloë are going after that Prince Valentine to the Rock of Eternity, aren't we, Chloë?

Dame I'm going nowhere. Not for a few minutes, anyway. My feet are killing me. I shall have to have a sit down.

Flop Me too.

Simon Oh, all right, then. But only for a few minutes.

Flip Look—there's an old log over there. Let's sit on that.

Flip and Flop drag in a "log" from the wings

Dame (*sitting on it and taking her shoes off*) Oh, that's lovely. Come on, everybody. Get settled down and we can have a little sing-song.

Simon (*sitting beside her*) All right. What shall we sing?

Flip and Flop sit one at each end of the log

Flip I know. "Don't sit on the stove, Granny, you're too old to ride the range."

Flop No, that's no good. Think of another.

Simon Shall we be singing bass or contralto?

Dame I don't know *either* of them. Are they from an opera?

Simon Oh, let's sing "Nellie Dean". We all know that.

They begin to sing

The Ghost enters and taps Flip on the shoulder. He looks up, sees it, screams and exits, chased by the Ghost

Dame (*stopping singing*) Here. There's no top "C" there . . . (*She looks for Flip*) Where's he gone?

Simon whispers in her ear

Well, he *would* eat those senna pods, wouldn't he?

Flop Let's get on with the song.

They sing

The Ghost enters and taps Flop. He looks up, screams and exits, chased by the Ghost

Simon (*noticing*) Hey. Hey, Chloë. *He*'s gone as well.

Dame (*stopping singing*) Eh? (*She looks around*) That's funny. Is it nearly time for the last bus? (*Coyly*) Still—it's better with just the two of us, isn't it? More cosy, like.

Simon reacts, and quickly begins singing again. Dame Durdon joins him trying to hold his hand

The Ghost enters and tickles Simon

Simon (*giggling*) Stoppit.
Dame Stop what?
Simon Tickling me.
Dame I didn't tickle you.
Simon Yes you did. You tickled my earhole. Right here. (*He indicates*)
Dame I didn't. You must have had a frigment of your menageration. Now come on and let's get on with the song.

They sing. The Ghost taps Dame Durdon on the shoulder. She looks at Simon, and pushes him gently. Simon looks surprised and pushes her back. She pushes harder still and Simon falls off the log

Simon Here. What was that for?
Dame You pushed me.
Simon No I didn't.
Dame Yes you did.
Simon I didn't. (*To the audience*) Did I kids? (*Ad lib with the audience*)
Dame Well somebody did, and there's only us two here.
Simon Oh, forget it, and let's get on with the song.

They sing again. The Ghost pushes Dame Durdon again

Dame (*rising*) That's done it. (*She rolls up her sleeves*)
Simon (*startled*) Wazzermarrer?
Dame I warned you about hitting me.
Simon I didn't. I never touched you. (*Ad lib with the audience*)
Dame We'd better have a look round.

They tiptoe round. The Ghost follows them

Simon (*to the audience*) There's nobody there at all. (*Ad lib*)
Dame Oh, take no notice of them, Simon. They're all drunk. Let's get on with the song.

They sit again and start to sing. The Ghost taps Simon who turns and sees it. He nods to it, continues singing for a moment, then realizes

With a loud scream Simon jumps up and dashes off

Simon—come back. Oh—he's gone. I'm all alone. By myself. Nobody else with me. On my own. Isn't it lonely? I think I'd better sing on my own to stop myself getting scared.

The Dame begins to sing in a quavery tone. The Ghost taps her. She looks up at it

The Ghost gives a shriek of terror and dashes off

The Lights fade to a Black-out
The log is removed by Dame Durdon

SCENE 7

The Rock of Eternity

The stage is bare but for a few shrubs and the gigantic Rock of Eternity which towers into the sky. A secret door is in the centre of the rock. The lighting is blue and green

Valentine enters L, *sword in hand*

Valentine Am I too late? (*He looks down at the floor*) No. There are no sign of footprints in the dust. I'll wait and ambush them. (*He hides behind the Rock*)

The King and Dilly enter

King What on earth did you drag me up here for? There's nothing to see around *this* place.
Dilly Oh, but there's a lovely view from the top. And besides—it's nice and quiet up here. No-one ever comes this way and we can have a nice little tête-à-tête.
King I don't want a tête-à-tête. I want my daughter and my Magic Crown.
Dilly But it's a romantic setting.
King (*snorting*) Romantic setting. The only romantic settings you know anything about are the ones with diamonds in them.
Dilly (*hurt*) Oh, Ferdinand. How could you? Don't tell me you've forgotten about the summer-house at the Palace of Dum.
King The summer-house at the Palace of . . . (*He clears his throat*) What about it?
Dilly Well that was a romantic setting, wasn't it? You went down on one knee to propose to me.
King No I did not. I was tying my shoelace.
Dilly And then you jumped up and flung your arms around me.
King I was stung by a wasp.
Dilly Then we played that game of yours. The one you invented.
King Game? (*He remembers*) Ah, yes. The game. What was it called now? (*He thinks*) Oh, yes. Photography. That was it. Photography.
Dilly We put out the lights to see what developed.
King (*coming back to the present*) But that was a *long* time ago Dilly. Things are different now. (*He remembers again*) But we *did* have fun, didn't we? All those years ago.
Dilly We did. And I can remember it as if it were only yesterday.

SONG EIGHTEEN

At the end of the song, Dilly flings her arms around the King

Ferdinand.

Valentine comes from behind the rock

Valentine Mother!
Dilly (*startled*) Valentine!
King Saved. (*He mops his brow*)
Valentine What are *you* doing here?
Dilly Oh, it was Ferdy's idea to come.
King Mine? But I never——
Dilly —expected anyone else to be here. He wanted to be alone with me.
King (*protesting*) I didn't want——
Dilly —anyone to know our little secret.
King Secret? *What* secret?
Dilly Our *wedding*, of course. (*She flutters*)
King Wedding? *Our* wedding?
Dilly (*to Valentine*) You see? It's so secret, even Ferdinand didn't know about it.
Valentine Well you can't stay out here. You don't seem to realize how dangerous it is.
King (*weakly*) I'm just beginning to find out.

Dilly playfully pushes him and he staggers

Dilly Whoopsy-daisy.
King (*to Valentine*) Kindly inform your mother . . .
Dilly Dilly to you, dear.
King And don't call me dear. I haven't got antlers.
Dilly No. But you've got your points. (*She pushes him again*)
Valentine You don't understand, Mother. We're all in great danger.
Dilly Why? Is there a tax-man hiding near us?
Valentine Do be serious, Mother. The Witch will be here at any moment.
Dilly Which witch?
Valentine Watt.
Dilly I said which witch?
Valentine I know. It's Witch Watt.
Dilly What?
Valentine That's right.
Dilly What's right?
Valentine Watt is.
Dilly (*baffled*) I don't know, dear. That's what I'm trying to find out.
Valentine Oh, I'll explain later, Mother. Now hide yourselves. Quickly.
Dilly Why?
Valentine I do wish you'd *listen*. The Witch has kidnapped Rosemary, and we're trying to rescue her from the Witch's clutches.
Dilly Witch's crutches? Has she broken her leg, then?
King Rosemary *kidnapped*? I won't allow it.
Valentine There's nothing we can do about it unless we hide before the Witch gets here.
Dilly Which witch?
Valentine Witch *Watt*.

Dilly Who?
King Oh, don't start all *that* again.
Valentine (*looking off*) Here she comes now. Hide.

The King and Valentine hide behind the rock

Dilly Who's coming? (*She looks round*) Valentine? You still haven't told me which Witch . . .

A hand comes from behind the rock and gags her, dragging her backwards out of view

The Witch and Rosemary enter L

Witch Behold. There stands the Enchanted stone
In silent majesty; alone.
And now by charms and Witch's pow'r,
The Rock I'll open this very hour.
Then once you're in, I'll close the door
To keep you trapped for evermore.
Rosemary Then do your worst. But I promise you that whatever happens to me will be nothing compared to what Valentine will do to you.
Witch (*snarling*) Valentine. Valentine. All I hear is Valentine.
Once rid of you, I'll deal with him.
His doom I'll seal. His wings I'll trim.
But now, enough. The spell I'll start
To bid the Great Rock's doors to part.

She raises her broom high

By blackest curse of demon's haunt.
By evil's powers, who good doth flaunt.
By shriek of fear and cry of pain,
I bid thee open once again.

The Lights dim

Come spirits from the hot earth's core
And force apart the granite door.
Then when inside, someone should stray . . .
Seal fast, forever. Forever, I say.

There is a loud rumbling noise as the rock opens to reveal a gloomy cave. The Witch drags Rosemary towards the opening

And now inside my Princess fine.
This very hour, triumph is *mine*. (*She shrieks with laughter*)

Valentine steps out of hiding, his sword in his hand

Valentine (*loudly*) Not so fast you old hag!

The Witch releases Rosemary with shock and recognizes Valentine

Witch Valentine!

Valentine Prepare to meet your doom.

Rosemary rushes to the King and Dilly as they emerge. Valentine advances on the Witch

Witch A thousand curses. I must fly.
But I'll return—by-and-by.

The Witch whirls around and heads off L, *but is prevented by the entrance of Rollo and his men who have their swords drawn. Quickly she turns and rushes in the other direction, but Dame Durdon, Simon, Flip and Flop block her way. All hold sticks or other weapons. The Witch backs away from them*

Valentine Not this time, my fine feathered friend. This time you stay.

Witch (*snarling*) Then fight we shall. Unto the death.
Come, Valentine. Draw your last breath.

Using her broom as a weapon, she hurls herself at Valentine, who evades her

One touch of this, and you die.

As the others all watch with bated breath, the Witch and Valentine do battle. Suddenly Valentine slips

I win. (*With a shout of triumph she lunges at him with her broom*)

Valentine (*rolling aside and stabbing her*) Not yet, you don't.

With a shriek of pain, the Witch staggers backwards and falls into the cave. With a crash, the great doors close on her. All cheer

Rosemary Valentine. (*She runs to him and embraces him*)

Valentine (*to all*) The Witch is dead. And now to return to the palace and prepare for our wedding day.

All cheer again. Dame Durdon hands the Crown to Ferdinand who puts it on. Dilly congratulates him. All congratuate one another

Fairy Gossamer enters R *in a white light*

Fairy Brave Valentine, now claim your bride.
You've won your fight. The Witch has died.
No remnant of her evil shows;
Young Lucy has regained her nose.
The King has back his Crown and money,
So Dilly will have lots of honey.
The Witch's castle, gold and land
Will go to Rollo and his band,
Whilst Flip and Flop who in their way
Have helped you—ev'ry single day
Shall have from me a brand new quip.
For Simon? Just a little tip.
Take courage. Take Dame Durdon's hand.

She'll make you proudest in the land.
Dame Durdon, for the part you played—
Of ev'ry fairy gift arrayed—
What choose you? Beauty, Wealth,
Wisdom, Patience, Youth or Health?

Dame Well—I can't see myself with a massive great diamon'—
So if you don't really mind, love—I'll just take Simon.

Fairy So be it. Then now to the Palace away.
Where we'll meet once more on your wedding day.

Everyone embraces his or her partner with much cheering, etc., as—

the CURTAIN *falls*

SCENE 8

A Corridor in the Palace

A song sheet—or interlude as required

SCENE 9

The Throneroom of the Palace

As the Finale music starts, the Blackbirds dance into the set, doing a cross twin circle and finishing each side of the staircase. After they take their bow, the Finale continues as follows—

Choristers
Rollo and Zorika
The Chamberlain and Lucy
Fairy Gossamer and Witch Watt
Flip and Flop
King Ferdinand and Queen Dilly
Dame Durdon and Simple Simon
Prince Valentine and Princess Rosemary

CURTAIN

FURNITURE AND PROPERTY LIST

ACT I

Scene 1

On stage: Bakery flat
Small wooden bridge

Off stage: Scroll and bell **(Chamberlain)**
Roller skates **(Dilly)**
Window frame **(Dilly)**
Wicker flower-basket **(Rosemary)**
Small coin **(Simon)**
Balloons, traders' goods, etc. **(Crowd)**

Scene 2

Off stage: Crystal ball, bag of rye **(Witch)**

Scene 3

On stage: Table. *On it:* bowls, spoons, flour, rolling-pin, mock pastry, large tin marked "Currants", small hand-brush, packet of soap powder
Large oven

Off stage: List **(Dame)**
Jam jar on strings, child's fishing-rod **(Simon)**
Baking bowl **(Dame)**
Handkerchief **(Valentine)**

Scene 4

Off stage: Suitcase containing giant mouse-trap **(Dilly)**
Watch in silver foil **(Dame)**
4 pound notes **(Simon)**
Handbag and mirror **(Dame)**
Clothes-basket **(Lucy)**

Scene 5

On stage: The Pie, concealed behind screen
Throne, black feather set near it

Off stage: Various foods on trays **(Footmen)**
Dead leaves **(King Ferdinand)**

Scene 7

On stage: Dressing-table
Rickety collapsible bed. *Under it:* large night-cap with patterned edge
2 candles in holders **(Dilly, Dame)**
Giant hairy spider

ACT II

Scene 1

Off stage: Sword **(Valentine)**

Scene 3

On stage: Log fire with cauldron and long stirring-spoon
Knives **(Gypsies)**
"Rattlesnake" **(Dame)**
Broom **(Witch)**

Scene 5

On stage: Throne
Off stage: Swords **(Knights)**

Scene 6

Off stage: Log seat **(Flip, Flop)**

Scene 7

On stage: Rock
Shrubs

Scene 8

On stage: Song sheet (or as required)

EFFECTS PLOT

ACT I

Cue 1 **Dilly** exits on skates (Page 1)
Loud glass crash

Cue 2 **King**: "Too late." (Page 22)
Roll of thunder

Cue 3 **Rosemary**: ". . . going to happen to us now." (Page 24)
2 claps of thunder

ACT II

Cue 4 Rock door opens (Page 54)
Loud rumbling noise

LIGHTING PLOT

Note: The following plot indicates those lighting changes and effects specified in text. These may be elaborated at the discretion of the director

Property fittings required: nil
Various simple interior and exterior settings

ACT I

To open:	Bright overall lighting	
Cue 1	As SCENE 2 opens *Blue light on backcloth, green spot on* **Witch**	(Page 7)
Cue 2	**Fairy** enters *White spot on* **Fairy**: *fade on her exit*	(Page 7)
Cue 3	**Witch**: "The Magic Crown is *mine!*" *Black-out*	(Page 8)
Cue 4	As SCENE 3 opens *Bring up interior of Bakery lighting*	(Page 8)
Cue 5	**Dame**: ". . . to do with this lot?" *Green spot on* **Witch**: *fade as she exits*	(Page 10)
Cue 6	**Dame** faints *Black-out*	(Page 14)
Cue 7	As SCENE 4 opens *Green spot on* **Witch**: *fade as she exits*	(Page 14)
Cue 8	**King** enters *Bring up Palace Corridor lighting*	(Page 14)
Cue 9	**Witch** enters during dance *Green spot on* **Witch**	(Page 17)
Cue 10	**Fairy** enters *White spot on* **Fairy**	(Page 17)
Cue 11	**Fairy**: "I banish you with light!" *Cross-fade from green to white spot on* **Witch**: *fade as she exits*	(Page 17)
Cue 12	**Fairy** exits *Fade white spot*	(Page 18)
Cue 13	**Chamberlain** and **Simon** exit *Bring up full lighting for Banqueting Hall*	(Page 21)
Cue 14	**King**: "Too late." *Lights flicker*	(Page 22)
Cue 15	**Rosemary**: ". . . going to happen to us now." *Lightning flashes*	(Page 24)
Cue 16	**Valentine**: ". . . find the Blackbirds' nest." *White spot on* **Fairy**: *fade as she exits*	(Page 25)
Cue 17	**Dame**: "Nothing ever happens here." *Black-out*	(Page 26)
Cue 18	As SCENE 6 opens *Bring up front lighting*	(Page 26)
Cue 19	As CURTAIN rises on SCENE 7 *Fade to dim, sinister light from Haunted Bedroom*	(Page 26)
Cue 20	**Witch** enters *Green spot on* **Witch**	(Page 29)

ACT II

To open:	Full overall lighting	
Cue 21	**Dame** and **Simon** exit *Green spot on* **Witch**: *fade as she exits*	(Page 35)
Cue 22	**Fairy** enters *White spot on* **Fairy**: *fade as she exits*	(Page 35)
Cue 23	As SCENE 2 opens *Bring up front lighting*	(Page 36)
Cue 24	As SCENE 3 opens *Bring up general lighting on Encampment: very colourful*	(Page 36)
Cue 25	As SCENE 4 opens *Fade to front lighting*	(Page 42)
Cue 26	As SCENE 5 opens *Bring up Witch's Lair lighting—dark and gloomy*	(Page 43)
Cue 27	As SCENE 6 opens *Bring up front lighting*	(Page 46)
Cue 28	**Lucy** and **Chamberlain** exit *Dim all lighting*	(Page 47)
Cue 29	**Valentine** enters with Crown *Return to Cue 27*	(Page 48)
Cue 30	**Fairy** enters *White spot on* **Fairy**: *fade as she exits*	(Page 48)
Cue 31	**Ghost** dashes off *Black-out*	(Page 51)
Cue 32	As SCENE 7 opens *Bring up general lighting for Rock of Eternity scene: green and blue predominating*	(Page 52)
Cue 33	**Witch**: ". . . open once again." *Dim all lighting*	(Page 54)
Cue 34	Doors close on **Witch** *Return to previous lighting*	(Page 55)
Cue 35	**Fairy** enters *White spot on* **Fairy**	(Page 55)
Cue 36	As SCENE 8 opens *Bring up spot on Song Sheet, or as required*	(Page 56)
Cue 37	As SCENE 9 opens *Bring up all lighting to full brightness for Finale*	(Page 56)

PRINTED IN GREAT BRITAIN BY
LATIMER TREND & COMPANY LTD PLYMOUTH
MADE IN ENGLAND